THE MANY FACES OF JUDAISM

Orthodox, Conservative, Reconstructionist & Reform

STUDENT WORKBOOK

BY MOSHE BEN AHARON

D1524864

BEHRMAN HOUSE, INC.

Acknowledgments

I would like to express my gratitude to several people who have helped me prepare this Workbook: Adam Bengal, managing editor of Behrman House, who coordinated its production with his characteristic blend of efficiency and gentle humor; John Simmons, who read the original manuscript, and made so many improvements; and Ms. Marva R. Hilliard—so conscientious, so professional, so patient—who typed, and retyped the manuscript.

And I particularly thank Seymour Rossel, who has worked with me through every stage of this project—editing, discussing, criticizing, and creating guidelines. His contributions, as usual, have been countless, varied, and indispensable.

Dedication

To Ralph Danis and Rabbi George Ende,
great educators and valued friends.

Book designed by Shiah Grumet

5
ISBN 0-87441-332-X

Manufactured in the United States of America

AMERICAN JUDAISM

A MEDIA MIX

This chapter tells about personalities and events over a period of more than three centuries. If these people and events were a part of our own time, their stories would be presented by the mass media—television, radio, newspapers and magazines—in the form of quiz shows, editorials, headlines, and interviews. Take a small leap of imagination, and try to discover which personality or event from the chapter belongs to each of the media presentations below.

1. News Headline

"GOLDEN DOOR" SLAMMED SHUT BY CONGRESS!
MISS LIBERTY WEEPS!

2. Editorial

The truth is, we don't like the Jews any better than the next fellow. But aren't we trying to have it both ways here? If our side wins, we call the Jews cowards who can't fight their own battles and have to pay Christians to protect them. If the Jews win, we call them pushy.

3. Television News Report

"Ladies and gentlemen, how can I describe this scene? It's eerie, even though it seems respectable. This is a court of law, not the Spanish Inquisition. And the judge, as near as I can tell, is not a religious fanatic.

"Yet, the result might be very much the same. Death! A man sentenced to die, not because of something he has done, but because of something he believes in!"

---

4. Interview

Q. Okay, you are here now. Everyone admires your courage and your pioneering spirit. What do you hope to accomplish?

A. Plainly put, a rescue mission. I'm here to save souls. I don't mean to sound dramatic or self-important, but the statistics here are pretty alarming. Intermarriage is on the rise, synagogue attendance is falling off, and Sabbath observance is fast becoming a disaster area.

Q. Do you intend to stay?

A. I do, indeed! It is lovely here. But it is frustrating. It's far away from the centers of Jewish life and learning. But I see myself as the first of many. That is my hope.

---

5. Quiz Show—"Name That Event"

Clue: "I sparked the largest Jewish immigration ever to the United States." Mystery event #1 is

---

Clue: "I am controversial. I am still bitterly opposed by some Christian groups, but generally applauded by Jewish leaders. I managed to take religion right out of the public schools in the United States." Mystery event #2 is

---

Clue: "I am a small, but in Jewish terms, highly important historical happening—a flight from religious persecution to the shores of a country that might turn out to be either a promised land or the same old nightmare. Those who took part were very few—but they were first!" Mystery event #3 is

---

POSSIBLE OR PRECISE?*

Circle the letter before the ending that *precisely*, rather than just possibly, completes each of the statements below.

1. The Naturalization Act of 1740 was important because it

    a. made for greater understanding among the various ethnic and religious groups that settled in the New World; **b.** angered many church officials by not forcing immigrants to take a Christian oath; **c.** sparked arguments between the Jews living in England and those who settled in the American colonies; **d.** offered immigrants to the New World an opportunity to become full–fledged British citizens; **e.** frustrated the efforts of those who preached and promoted anti-Semitism.

2. The wave of Jewish immigration that came to America directly before and after World War II and the German Holocaust

    a. greatly improved the quality of American Jewish religious life and culture; **b.** served as a grim reminder to American Jews that a pogrom, or even a Holocaust, could happen here; **c.** settled mainly in big cities with large Jewish populations, rather than in small towns; **d.** did not readily mingle with American Jews who had settled here a generation or two earlier; **e.** were only a tiny fraction of European Jewry, the vast majority of whom perished in the Holocaust.

3. The fact that only 50 percent of all Jews in America are members of a synagogue shows that

    a. religion does not easily flourish in a modern, technologically advanced, consumer culture; **b.** belief in God does not necessarily lead to membership in a synagogue (or church); **c.** it was far easier to be an observant Jew in nineteenth century eastern Europe than it is in twentieth century America; **d.** a lack of Jewish education leads to a lack of interest in Jewish religious and cultural life; **e.** American Jews are assimilating in greater numbers and at a swifter rate today than ever before.

4. The American Constitution, with its all-important Bill of Rights

    a. guaranteed the permanent separation of church and state, and made freedom of religion the law of the land; **b.** helped to discourage anti-Semitism in this country; **c.** is the major reason why American Jews have been mayors, governors, senators, Supreme Court Justices, and Secretaries of State; **d.** served as a model for other countries that wished to rid themselves of anti-Semitic laws, customs, and attitudes; **e.** caused a backlash of anti-Semitic hostility on the part of Christian Americans who believed that American Jews were receiving too much, too soon.

5. The 1963 Supreme Court decision on prayers in public schools

   a. caused fear among some Jews that they would be accused of "getting God kicked out of the public schools;" **b.** unified rabbis, priests, and ministers, all of whom were against this decision; **c.** has not yet succeeded in removing all religious observances from the schools; **d.** has resulted in less religious interest, or awareness, among young Americans today than ever before; **e.** was hailed by many Jewish leaders as a major victory for religious freedom and equality.

6. The story of Peter Stuyvesant's conflict with the Jews demonstrates that

   a. anti-Semitic attitudes were as common among the rich, powerful, and privileged as they were among the poor; **b.** Jews have always been regarded as outsiders, wherever and whenever they have lived; **c.** Jews were barred from military service because they were considered weak and cowardly; **d.** Jews could sometimes gain ground and win rights even in societies where they were disliked, restricted, and regarded with suspicion; **e.** anti-Semitism was far less likely to flourish in the New World than in Europe.

7. The eastern European Jewish immigration to this country

   a. was dramatic proof that the Jewish people never really felt at home in Russia and Poland; **b.** was a source of anxiety and embarrassment to the Jews of German and Sephardic origin who had already been living here in America decades or generations; **c.** was mainly responsible for the fact that American Jewish life took a sharp turn toward traditional Judaism after more than a century of drifting in the opposite direction; **d.** demonstrated the importance of Yiddish to the creation of a strong Jewish community; **e.** saved the existing American Jewish community from disintegration and extinction.

8. In general, the American Jewish experience teaches that

   a. Judaism does best in a democracy; **b.** Jewish life cannot survive in the long run without rabbis, teachers, and scholars; **c.** when one great center of Jewish life disappears, another will rise to take its place; **d.** in a country made up of many immigrant groups and graced with a Bill of Rights guaranteeing freedom of religion, anti-Semitism is ultimately doomed; **e.** outside events often have a great influence upon the shape and direction of Jewish life.

TRUE OR FALSE—AND WHY?*

Look at the photographs on pages 11, 13, 14, 19, and 21 of the text, and the drawing on page 22, and read their captions. Then decide whether each of the statements below is true or false. In the space that follows—using the photographs and drawing as references—give a brief reason for your choice.

PHOTO STUDY

1. Many Jews who immigrated to the United States during the early and mid-nineteenth century began to feel socially at ease and economically secure in less than thirty years. **T F**

_____

_____

_____

2. Most of the Jewish immigrants from Eastern Europe who arrived here at the turn of the twentieth century worked long hours for little money. **T F**

_____

_____

_____

3. Because this was a new country, made up of many different groups of immigrants, Jews enjoyed equal rights and full citizenship from the very beginning. **T F**

_____

_____

_____

4. Eastern European Jews were willing to work and sacrifice well beyond their means so they could have what they considered a proper synagogue in their midst. **T F**

_____

_____

_____

5. Because they were students and scholars in eastern Europe, Jewish immigrants could not adapt to the strains and hardships of physical work in this country.   **T   F**

_____

_____

_____

6. Because the United States at the turn of the century was so busy, difficult, and demanding, the typical eastern European Jewish immigrant was young and unattached.   **T   F**

_____

_____

_____

7. At times, poverty could inspire a sense of closeness and cooperation within immigrant families.   **T   F**

_____

_____

_____

EVENTS AND EFFECTS*

Match the events in the left column with the effects that they helped bring about, in the right column. Make your choice by writing the number before the event in the box beside the matching effect.

1. The Holocaust

☐ Established the principles of religious freedom and the separation of church and state.

2. Winning the right for Jews to stand guard duty in New Amsterdam

☐ Was largely responsible for the first wave of Jewish immigration that came to these shores.

3. The creation of the state of Israel

☐ Was a small but important first step in the process of the American Jewish community's becoming religiously, culturally, and institutionally self-sufficient.

4. The Russian pogroms under Czar Alexander III, during the 1880s

☐ Created a precedent (the first of a number of steps) that paved the way for Jews in this country to achieve the status of equals among equals.

5. The Naturalization Act of 1740

☐ Brutally illustrated anti-Semitism's murderous potential, dramatically hastened the creation of the state of Israel, and ended the history of the European Jewish community as a great religious and cultural center.

6. The wave of eastern European Jews to this country

□ Laid the groundwork for developing rabbis, educators, and other Jewish professionals, who were born and bred in this country.

7. The Spanish Inquisition

□ Spurred the beginning of what would become a mass migration of Jews to this country, (and at the same time inspired a handful of young pioneers to go on aliyah to Palestine).

8. The ratification of the American Constitution

□ Gave Jews in this country a sense of equality, a sureness of political identity, and a tradition of belonging, which have helped shape our attitudes for over 200 years.

9. The establishment of Orthodox, Conservative, and Reform rabbinical schools in this country

□ Has given the Jews of the world, among other things, an address—a haven, a refuge, a place to go—in times of persecution and danger.

10. The immigration of Rabbi Abraham Rice to the United States in 1840

□ Revitalized Jewish life in the New World by a vast inpouring of the old ways.

HIDDEN WORD HUNT*

Eight Hebrew words or phrases are hidden in the block of letters below. They may be written vertically, horizontally or diagonally. They may begin at the beginning of a row or column, in the middle, or even creep around a corner. Sometimes the words share a letter. Circle the words or phrases when you find them. (Hint: All these words are mentioned in the chapter, and their English meanings are given in the list below.)

1. Charity (from the Hebrew word for righteousness and justice)
2. Commandments
3. A ritual bath
4. An unholy land
5. A formal community
6. Cantors
7. The Hebrew word for Saturday
8. Exile

K	G	H	A	Z	Z	A	N	I	M
U	E	S	H	A	B	B	A	T	I
L	G	H	B	R	A	M	E	D	K
T	A	M	I	T	Z	V	O	T	V
R	L	O	Y	L	P	E	R	M	E
E	U	V	C	I	L	S	M	O	H
F	T	X	Z	N	H	A	G	T	O
A	C	L	O	T	E	R	H	C	X
M	T	Z	E	D	A	K	A	H	B
E	D	I	N	A	H	J	P	M	T

There were four major waves of Jewish immigrants to this country: (1) the Sephardim, mostly from the West Indies, who took root during the seventeenth and eighteenth centuries (there were some Ashkenazim in this wave, but the Sephardim were the majority); (2) the western Europeans, mostly from Germany, Austria, France, and Italy, who fled here from their native lands during the first half of the nineteenth century for political reasons; (3) the eastern Europeans, some two and one-half million strong, who arrived on these shores between 1881 and 1924; (4) refugees from the Holocaust, who reached here either before 1940 or after the German defeat in 1945. And while the majority of Jewish immigrants came here for more or less the same reason—relief from religious and political persecution in their lands of origin—the experiences of the four immigrant groups in this country differed in many ways.

The passages below are imaginary entries from the diaries of Jewish immigrants. Try to identify the immigrant group to which each entry belongs. In the box after each passage, place the correct letter: **S** for the Sephardic wave; **W** for the western European wave; **E** for the eastern European wave; **H** for the Holocaust survivors.

1. "This is a strange land. So big and busy. So different from the old country. And it's so difficult to be a good Jew here, for all of the freedom and all of the opportunities to get ahead (or maybe because of them). Still, I shouldn't complain. There's work for me in the dress factory, and my children can get a good education, maybe even go to college. One thing is sure, my children won't have to live in a hot, crowded Lower East Side tenement—like we do. They'll have a better life than their mother and father." ☐

2. "My American relatives tell me to find comfort in the fact that because of what we went through, a Jewish state may soon come into being. Why can't they understand that nothing—nothing in the world!—begins to explain, much less justify, our ordeal?" ☐

3. "The thing is, there is a fundamental principle involved. I'm no soldier, and I hope to God that I'll never have to fight any more. But when the government tells me that I can't bear arms—that I have to pay money, instead, for someone else to protect me—what they are doing is making me a second class citizen all over again. And that I don't want. Not here! Let the New World be a new chapter in Jewish history—not a repeat of our life in Europe!" ☐

4. "Well, we are here! We'll set down our roots and create a community. And somehow we'll survive. We have to. But it will never be the same. Still, what I must keep in mind is that eastern European Jewish life has ceased to be. Our future, our hope, lies in America. This is the only country in which there is the possibility of a dynamic, creative, Jewish community such as once existed in Poland and Russia." ☐

5. "What a thrill! What an experience! What a famous first! I haven't seen a rabbi since I left Germany nearly twenty years ago! And to my children, a rabbi is someone out of a Jewish folktale, a relic from a remote, old-country past. Well, I admire that individual's guts, if not necessarily his wisdom. He's as much a pioneer in his way as those people who go out West in a covered wagon. Maybe more so—because he's so alone. The question is what can he do? How long will he last? And can one man—no matter how gifted and dedicated, really turn things around all by himself?" ☐

6. "What do I write home? That there's a synagogue every two blocks or so. And street after street where you hear only Yiddish. And a marketplace that looks like it was plucked directly from the old country. The only thing is, they must understand that you have to work hard and long here to make even a minimum living. The sweatshop is a real ingredient of the American Dream. And they would be doing themselves a big favor by banishing the term "Golden Land" from their vocabulary altogether." ☐

7. "I find it staggering, and yes, morally unbearable. It's like the continuation of a nightmare after a brief spurt of wakefulness. Not long ago, the nations of the world stood around and said nothing while a people was destroyed. Now they are standing around and saying nothing, while a whole state is in danger of being destroyed!" ☐

8. "This is absolute madness. I didn't leave my country because of religious persecution. I left because I was sick and tired of futile political causes and pointless wars. And so what do I find about to happen here? A war that will do no one any good. A war that will drive Jew to take up arms against Jew." ☐

9. "Look, let's not kid ourselves. Sure there's anti-Semitism—sometimes quite brutal. And there are plenty of people who would call this a Christian country, and label us non-Christian outsiders. But, it seems to me, there are three major differences here: first, we are all recent immigrants to this country—except for the Indians; second, the Jews are one of many ethnic and religious groups—rather than, say, a Jewish minority living among a French-Catholic

majority; third, and most important to my way of thinking, our rights of citizenship and equality are now being written into American law, not as an afterthought or amendment, but as a fundamental constitutional principle." ☐

10. "Wow! Talk about doing things backward! Only in America do we go, not from the Orthodox, or traditional, to the Reform, or modern, as some people would say, but vice-versa. And now, for the first time ever, there are in this country more Orthodox synagogues than Reform." ☐

PERSONAL DEFINITIONS

The Jews who immigrated to this country were searching for new meanings and definitions. The following sentences are incomplete. Give your own personal definitions to complete the sentences.

1. A good Jew is one who

2. A good Jewish family is one that

3. A good Jewish education should

4. A good Jewish community must

ORTHODOX JUDAISM

2

TRADITIONAL JUDAISM IN A NEW SETTING

WHO, WHAT, AND WHERE AM I?*

1. I am the first Orthodox rabbi to settle in the United States, and, quite frankly, was deeply discouraged about the future of traditional Judaism in this country.

_____

2. I am the youth movement of religious Zionism, named, by the way, after one of the great rabbis of ancient times.

_____

3. I am a major Orthodox university—though I started very small— that educates Jewish youth and trains future rabbis.

_____

4. I am known as an ultra-Orthodox religious organization, but I am of the firm opinion that most Orthodox groups are simply not Orthodox enough.

_____

5. I am a practice, originally borrowed from American Christians, that has become an important part of the Sabbath and festival services conducted by most Jewish congregations in this country.

_____

6. I am the organization that counts most American Orthodox synagogues among its membership.

_____

7. I am the leader of the largest Hasidic group in the United States, considered relatively modern, liberal, and dynamic—and roundly criticized by many of my fellow Hasidim, who consider themselves more pious.

_____

8. I am the agency that coordinates the majority of Orthodox day schools and yeshivot in the United States.

_____

9. We both helped create a great Orthodox university; both of us were its presidents.

_____ and _____

10. I am an organization—rooted in the American experience, rather than in old-country ways—to which the largest number of Orthodox rabbis in the United States belongs today.

_____

History can teach us many lessons. Most of the lessons below are taken directly from the chapter. In each statement, however, there is *one* lesson that does not come from the chapter. Find the "outsider" and circle its letter.

1. The story of Yeshiva University teaches that

   a. gifted and dedicated leadership often means the difference between an institution's success or its failure; **b.** the creation and development of a school, college, or university sometimes reflects the changing needs of the community which it serves; **c.** Orthodox leaders reject the belief that secular studies play an important role in the education of the Jewish young; **d.** a school, like an individual, is able to develop and grow constantly.

2. The account of Rabbi Samson Raphael Hirsch's life teaches that

   a. Orthodox rabbis can preach, teach, write, and engage in scholarship in a variety of languages other than Hebrew or Yiddish; **b.** political freedom, including the right to leave the ghetto and live wherever one pleases and participation in the surrounding non-Jewish culture, inevitably lead to assimilation; **c.** national boundaries need not be barriers to contact and communications between Jewish communities. The Jews in one country may maintain close ties with, and have a powerful influence upon, Jews in other countries; **d.** nineteenth century Orthodox rabbis regarded the loosening and liberalization of tradition, advocated by the Reform movement, as a great danger to Judaism.

3. The struggles of Rabbis Rice and Edelmar, in the years before the eastern European immigration to this country, teach that

   a. to further their belief in Jewish life, rabbis could be pioneers willing to strike out for parts unknown, to endure loneliness, to fight against overwhelming obstacles and stumbling blocks, and to suffer daily disappointment; **b.** Judaism is sometimes endangered, not only by anti-Semitism or assimilation, but by the life of a larger society; **c.** it is difficult, if not impossible, for a traditional Jewish community to survive upon belief alone. It needs to be nourished by education, religious institutions, and regular ritual observance; **d.** Orthodox Judaism cannot take root in a country marked by slavery, civil war, a wild frontier, and bloody battles with Indian tribes.

4. The way in which the Union of Orthodox Jewish Congregations came into being teaches that

a. Ashkenazic and Sephardic Orthodox Jews torn by differences of origin, Hebrew pronunciation, and ritual style simply cannot work together; **b.** the presence and growth of the Reform movement in the United States has, in a way, been a source of inspiration to American Orthodoxy, moving its leaders to take actions and directions that they might not have taken otherwise; **c.** modern Orthodox thinking actively embraces the pronouncement of the prophet Isaiah: "From out of Zion will the Law go forth, and the word of the Lord from Jerusalem." It views Judaism as a dynamic blending of nationhood and religious belief; **d.** grappling with questions of Jewish Law is a task that lies in the hands of both Orthodox professionals and lay people.

5. The various photographs in the chapter and in the special photo section beginning on page 38 teach that

   a. Jewish tradition has been widely and richly expressed through the arts for centuries; **b.** if an observant eighteenth century European Jew were transported via time machine to the present, he or she would find nothing familiar in the American Orthodox way of life; **c.** Orthodox Jews are not all alike; they may differ from one another in lifestyle, appearance, manner of dress, and relationship with the outside world; **d.** social and moral values are often woven into acts of ritual observance.

6. Among the qualities and values featured in the photographs are

   a. determined opposition to Reform Judaism; **b.** a love of learning for its own sake; **c.** kindness and compassion; **d.** close family ties.

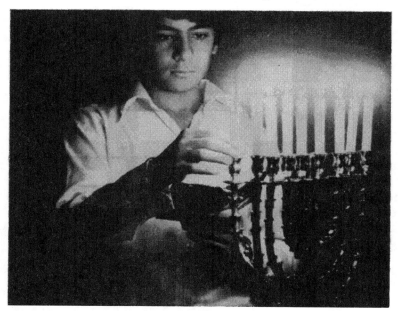

There are a number of Hebrew words, deeply rooted in Jewish life, tradition, and experience that have taken on special meanings, and cannot be translated directly into another language. Some of these words appear in this chapter. The illustrations and accompanying descriptions in the panel below attempt to capture these special meanings. In the space above each panel, write the Hebrew word that you think it expresses.

1. This individual, usually poorly paid but deeply dedicated, taught Jewish young people not how to make a living, but how to make a life, and bears a good deal of responsibility for American Jewish survival.

2. Strictly translated—a place to sit and study. This is the name given only to Orthodox day schools.

3. This word embraces acts of ritual observance, social responsibility, and moral concern. What all these acts have in common, according to Orthodox Judaism, is that they are commanded by God.

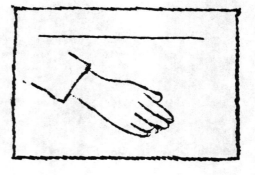

4. This ceremony takes place only after years of intensive study. It differs from other graduation ceremonies in that it demands of those who receive its title not only knowledge and understanding of subject matter, but commitment to a way of life.

5. This was the ghetto version of the American little red school house, where children of all ages would crowd together in a single room to learn "readin' and writin'" (in Hebrew), prayer, customs and ceremonies, and Jewish Law.

6. Laws that tell observant Jews what and when they may eat. These laws are far more easily followed in big cities than in small towns in this country.

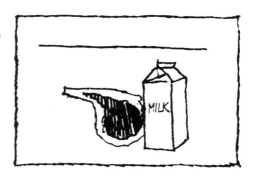

7. This is a value, rooted in our history and tradition, that takes precedence over even the most sacred rituals and ceremonies. It is regarded not so much as an act of giving as the fulfillment of Jewish moral obligation.

Match the imaginary but quite possible statements (from letters, journals, and the like) in the right column with the individuals—key personalities in the story of modern Orthodox Judaism—who might have made them in the left column. Make your choice by placing the number before the person in the blank beside the matching statement.

1. Rabbi Samson Raphael Hirsch

☐ "We have come a long way! Our college is the first of its kind in this country. Why do we offer secular studies, rather than a purely Jewish curriculum? Because our rabbis and our other students must understand the ways of the outside world. This is particularly important today, with Hitler and his gang of Nazis on the verge of taking power in Germany."

2. Dr. Samuel Belkin

☐ "Unity? Don't kid yourself! Jews, particularly those of the Orthodox variety, seem unable to unite. I am not knocking what we've just done, I wouldn't have accepted the presidency if I didn't believe in its importance."

3. The Lubavitcher Rebbe

☐ "People have called me a pioneer. Maybe so. I am the first of my profession to strike roots in the New World. But I frankly find it difficult to maintain my optimism—which is so necessary to the pioneer. This is a great country, but it's hard to be a Jew here."

4. Rabbi Bernard Revel

☐ "We have been forced to live in ghettoes for centuries, because of the ignorance and hatred of anti-Semites. This is no reason to make something holy out of the ghetto. Where are we commanded to withdraw from the world? Being a good observant Jew must be a matter of keeping the mitzvot, and guarding against the danger of the Reform movement, rather than worrying about length of beard and manner of dress."

5. Rabbi Abraham ☐ "It's hard to believe. A full-fledged university.
   Rice   Still, so much has happened during the years I
                         have occupied this office. The Nazi Holocaust.
                         The creation of Israel. Four Arab-Israeli wars.
                         The beginning of the Soviet Jewish exodus. The
                         development of a young, modern, dynamic Or-
                         thodoxy in the United States . . ."

6. Rabbi Henry ☐ "In a sense, my followers and I are caught
   Pereira Mendes   squarely in the middle—between a modern
                        world that thinks that we are quaint or even
                        slightly medieval, and those who share our way
                        of life, who accuse us of compromising or even
                        betraying our cherished principles. My beliefs
                        are rooted in the idea of joy—in prayer, in
                        study, in daily life."

THE ORTHODOX EXPERIENCE*

The following terms were among the main ingredients of the Orthodox
experience in the United States over a period of more than three centuries. Unscramble the letters and, where necessary, the word order.
(Example: MYFIAL A FELI GRONTS = FAMILY A LIFE STRONG =
A STRONG FAMILY LIFE.)

1. SLENOLEINS = _____

_____

2. NIZOMIS LOUREIGIS A ACTEERD = _____

_____

3. FO GIOSIRN TEVIRAY A = _____

_____

4. OT HENGAC POEN = _____

_____

5. GRALE NI TECISI CLATOED = _____

_____

6. NAYM THEYVOSI LIBUT = _____

_____

THEN AND TODAY . . .

1. Survival Scales

Until the beginning of the vast eastern European immigration in the 1880s, observant American Jews found it very difficult to practice their traditions and preserve their way of life. Nineteenth century United States was busy, bustling, demanding, and lacked large Jewish communities, educational facilities, and religious resources. In short, it was tough to be a Jew during most of the past century and—for different reasons—it is tough to be a Jew today.

The survival scales below are divided into two sets of "weights" for you to fill in as best you can. In the left set, (Column A) write down three things, within your community, that you think make it difficult to be an observant, educated, committed American Jew today. In the right set, (Column B) write down three things that you think work to strengthen and preserve American Jewish life today.

A   B

2. Tipping The Scales

A philanthropist has given you a $100,000 grant, to be used to promote Jewish survival in your community in whatever way you judge to be most effective. In the form of specific, practical suggestions, how would you use this money to help tip the scales in favor of American Jewish survival?

_____

_____

_____

_____

3. A Survival Strategy

One of the large dangers that confronted observant American Jews during most of the nineteenth century was the problem of isolation. There were simply too few Jews, scattered over too vast an area. The inpouring of eastern European immigrants dramatically changed this picture for the better in an incredibly brief time, demonstrating that—at least insofar as Jewish communal life was concerned—quantity could help bring about quality. Imagine that you, as an adult, are to be similarly isolated; that for professional reasons, you and your husband or wife and children must settle in an area where there is no Jewish community, no educational or religious resources for several hundred miles in any direction. You are spiritually set adrift. How would you chart a survival strategy to live as Jews, and for your children to grow up with a deep sense of Jewish identity and commitment? On the rungs of the ladder below, set down what you believe are elements of a survival strategy in their order of importance, from top to bottom.

MOST IMPORTANT

4. A Survival Curriculum

Another lesson learned from the experience of our immigrant ancestors from Russia and Poland was the central importance of a good education to a flourishing Jewish life and tradition. Imagine that you are in charge of a class of eight-year-olds. To train them Jewishly you have two hours a week on Sunday morning. During those two hours you may teach whatever subject, or subjects, you wish. Which subject or subjects would you choose, and why?

SUBJECT	REASON

ORTHODOX JUDAISM BELIEFS AND PRACTICES

3

TRUE OR FALSE?*

"True or False?" is a well-known and widely used ingredient of student activity books. It has a special aim in this instance—to correct many of the mistaken ideas that people have had about Orthodox Judaism over the years. A careful reading of this chapter will help you answer these "True or False" statements.

1. Though united in belief, Orthodox leaders have sometimes disagreed with one another on issues of major importance. **T F**

2. Most Orthodox Jews believe that religious values should play an active role in the laws and lifestyle of the state of Israel. **T F**

3. Orthodox Judaism does not permit divorce, because of the importance that it places upon family life. **T F**

4. Orthodox Jews vigorously resist even minor changes in ritual and prayer, because, among other reasons, they fear that this could weaken Jewish identity and tradition. **T F**

5. Men and women are not allowed to sit together in an Orthodox shul, because women have virtually no role in synagogue worship. **T F**

6. Ultra-Orthodox Jews do not believe that the idea of Eretz Yisrael, the Land of Israel, is a key element in Jewish tradition today. **T F**

7. Many liberal Orthodox leaders believe that at times, Jewish tradition must be aware of, and open to, change.   **T F**

8. Liberal Orthodox rabbis today do not generally believe that the Torah is the revealed word of God, but will not say so openly because of their desire to keep the Jewish religion strong and intact.   **T F**

9. In the Orthodox scheme of things, Jewish law must be applied strictly in the home, the synagogue, and the community, but has no place in the business or professional world.   **T F**

10. Most Orthodox leaders believe that the religious differences between Jews and Christians are fundamental and run deep, and will not be papered over by pious sentiments or pretty words.   **T F**

11. In order to sustain their way of life, Orthodox Jews in this country have become involved in politics.   **T F**

ODD IDEA OUT*

This chapter discusses many attitudes and ideas. Each of the statements below possess several sections—one of which is an "odd idea out." Either it is not covered in the chapter or it is not true. Circle the letter before the section that should not be there.

1. Being "Torah-true" means that

   a. you believe that the Torah is not a creation of human beings, but was revealed by God to His chosen people at Mount Sinai more than 3,000 years ago; **b.** you do not pick and choose which laws to obey and which to ignore; **c.** you must avoid those who do not share your Orthodox lifestyle; **d.** you cannot place ethical laws above ritual laws in order of importance; all laws revealed by God must be regarded as equal.

2. On the question of establishing a relationship with the Christian clergy:

   a. many Orthodox rabbis remain highly suspicious of Christian intentions; **b.** Orthodox Judaism draws a sharp line between Catholics and Protestants because the Vatican has never formally recognized the state of Israel; **c.** one stumbling block to communication is the lingering Christian belief that the Jews are responsible for Jesus's death; **d.** some Orthodox leaders think that Jews and Christians should create a middle ground of mutual secular concerns in which they might cooperate, but should leave religious issues strictly alone.

3. The idea of the chosen people

   a. has been largely abandoned by liberal Orthodox Jews; **b.** has been expressed not only in our history and culture, but in our prayers, as well; **c.** has been pointed to by some Jews as proof of our superiority to other peoples; **d.** has been interpreted by most Jews as a call to high moral standards, strict ritual observance, and the role of spiritual educator to other nations.

4. In their attitudes toward religious practices, Orthodox Jews may be said to

   a. regard them not as a scattering of rituals to be observed on special occasions, but as a total way of life; **b.** make a strenuous effort to pass on their beliefs and way of life to their children; **c.** have totally resisted the forces of modernization and change; **d.** carry the laws of the Torah into the everyday life of the business world.

5. In its ideas about God, Orthodox Judaism

   a. would feel very much at home in the Jewish world of one hundred, or even one thousand, years ago; **b.** demands proof of God's existence or insights into God's nature; **c.** has difficulty explaining the existence of evil in the world; **d.** has generally shied away from trying to make religious or moral sense of the Holocaust.

6. Rabbi Berkovits's concept of "authentic Judaism"

   a. recognizes change as a fact of life, and argues that Jewish law must change to meet new realities; **b.** is keenly attuned to the everyday needs of people, and to the social issues of the day; **c.** has addressed itself to the danger of a growing distance and lack of communication between Orthodox scholars (rabbis, teachers, etc.) and the people at large; **d.** rejects scholarship and study as the main ingredients of the Jewish lifestyle, and insists that they be replaced by a strong sense of compassion and an active concern for people.

7. On the question of *halachah*:

   a. there is sharp disagreement, even among Orthodox leaders, as to the need for such law in the modern world; **b.** it has been pointed out that even the simplest ritual has a higher—sometimes hidden—moral meaning; **c.** some rabbis see it as a spiritual discipline that keeps us from thinking too much of ourselves, and grants us a broader, nobler view of our place and purpose in this world; **d.** it has been suggested that observance of its laws bring us in close touch with the rhythms of nature and the secrets of the universe.

WORDS AND MEANINGS*

Some of the most important features of Jewish tradition are widely known by their Hebrew (and occasionally Yiddish) names. Match the meanings below with the Hebrew words that they express, found in the chapter.

1. A Jewish divorce, the only one recognized by Orthodox rabbis.

   _____

2. An Orthodox court of law.

   _____

3. The act of being called to the Torah, a word that also means immigration to Israel.

   _____

4. The object that separates men and women in an Orthodox synagogue.

   _____

5. The great religious scholars and educators of a particular time period.

   _____

6. The skull cap, worn by males for religious reasons. Its Yiddish name is generally more well-known.

   _____ or _____
         (Hebrew)   (Yiddish)

7. The traditional prayerbook, the name of which comes from the same Hebrew root word as the ceremonial feast that ushers in the holiday of *Pesah*, or Passover.

   _____

8. The individual, schooled in both medical procedure and strict Jewish ritual, who performs the act of circumcision.

   _____

9. The Code of Jewish Law that serves as a constant, ever-present network of moral and religious guidelines.

_____

10. The daily prayer or mourning offered for a parent, a husband, a wife, a child, or other close relatives, which is, in fact, an affirmation of faith.

_____

11. The system of laws which governs the daily behavior of religious Jews.

_____

12. The ritual bath attended by Orthodox women.

_____

PHOTO STUDY*

The photographs in this chapter (on pages 45, 47, 50, 52), and their captions, teach us a number of things, as listed here. Circle the letter before the statement below that does *not* belong with the others.

A. Religious styles, customs and rituals may differ—even among Orthodox Jews.

B. Physical beauty can be a valued feature of Orthodox ritual.

C. Differences in religious practices among the Orthodox may be outgrowths of the fact that the Jewish people were dispersed to a variety of countries and cultures.

D. Orthodox Judaism can be found in the suburbs, as well as in the big cities of this country.

E. Orthodox rabbis are generally better educated than their Conservative, Reform, or Reconstructionist counterparts.

F. Orthodox Jews represent a wide assortment of cultural backgrounds, economic levels, geographical locations, and architectural tastes.

LOOKING FOR UNDERSTANDING

The questions below offer important keys to understanding Orthodox Judaism. Answer them briefly and clearly.

1. What, exactly, is the meaning of "Torah-true?"

_____

_____

_____

2. Why does the Holocaust pose a particularly painful and difficult problem for Orthodox Judaism?

_____

_____

_____

3. How does Eretz Yisrael (the Land of Israel) differ from the state of Israel (Medinat Yisrael) and how is this difference expressed by the ultra-Orthodox minority?

_____

_____

_____

4. Why does Orthodox Judaism not accept people who convert in order to marry Jews?

_____

_____

_____

5. Why have the Orthodox lagged behind the Conservative, Reform, and Reconstructionist movements in such modern innovations as the Bat Mitzvah ceremony for girls?

_____

_____

_____

WORD SCRAMBLE*

Each of the seven scrambled words below is an important element of Orthodox Jewish belief and practice. Unscramble them. Place the correct words in the boxes that follow. Then, unscramble the ten circled letters, to reveal something that most Orthodox Jews share, at least in their approach to their tradition.

1. **DYTUS**

2. **NALD**

3. **REPARY**

4. **TIHAF**

5. **SHIECT**

6. **TAIRUL**

7. **MAYFIL**

THE QUESTION OF EVIL

ISSUE

1. Challenge

As the chapter points out, one of the most troublesome questions facing Jewish religious thinkers today is the presence of evil in the world. Especially in modern times, science and technology have made it easier for human beings to cause suffering and pain, and to destroy. Imagine that someone has asked you the question: "How can you still speak of an all-knowing and all-powerful God when you know that six million Jews died in the German Holocaust?" How would you answer?

_____

_____

_____

_____

_____

_____

2. The World Today

Nor has evil ended since the Holocaust. In the space below, list three or four of the worst evils that you see in the world around you today.

_____

_____

_____

_____

_____

3. Most Frightening

Which of the above examples of evil do you think is the most frightening—and why?

_____

_____

_____

_____

_____

REFORM JUDAISM
THE MOVEMENT FOR JEWISH REFORM

4

HISTORICAL LESSONS*

The statements below contain a number of historical lessons drawn directly from the text. Each statement contains one section that is an "outsider"—it is false. Circle the letter before the section that is false.

1. An examination of the eight-point program of the Pittsburgh Platform teaches that

   a. nineteenth century Reform Judaism placed great emphasis upon individual morality and social responsibility; **b.** Reform thinking of that period generally rejected Jewish ritual practices and supernatural beliefs; **c.** Reform Jews largely saw anti-Semitism as a product of an era long past, which certainly posed no serious threat to the modern American Jewish community; **d.** nineteenth century Reform Judaism did not accept the idea that the Jewish people, unlike Catholics and Protestants, were a nation as well as a religion.

2. The early history of the Reform movement teaches that

   a. what begins as an effort to modernize tradition may ultimately lead to the creation of a new religious movement; **b.** nineteenth century German Reform leaders hoped that the changes that they were working to bring about would encourage assimilation.; **c.** the early

34

Reform leaders looked upon Protestant and Catholic churches as spiritual competition, and regarded the Jewish people as a religious market, an audience to be fought for and won; **d.** some Reform leaders believed that for many Jews, Hebrew could be a stumbling block to understanding.

3. Isaac Mayer Wise's career teaches that

   a. a gifted, dedicated individual might shape and direct the Jewish future; **b.** an important building block of a religious movement is a special college equipped to train clergymen and teachers along the lines of its particular beliefs, values, and world outlook; **c.** at times, history may take a different course because of a single error in judgment, or a freak accident; **d.** without Wise's achievements, the Reform movement would have withered and died once the largely Yiddish-speaking Orthodox eastern European Jewish immigrants began pouring into this country.

4. The publication of *The Gates of Prayer, The Gates of the House*, and *The Gates of Repentance* teaches that

   a. the Hebrew language is an important key to Jewish identity and tradition, even for those who cannot speak it fluently; **b.** the Reform movement has shown itself capable of continuing change, and of acknowledging and correcting past errors; **c.** at times, history does not move steadily and surely in a single direction, but, rather, is marked by uneven zigs and zags—and yesterday's notion of "old fashioned" or "obsolete" may well be considered a bold vision of the future by today's standards; **d.** many Jews seem to cherish and need the rituals and ceremonies of their religion.

5. The story of Stephen S. Wise teaches that

   a. Judaism is most likely to flourish in large centers of Jewish population; **b.** Zionism has become a central part of Jewish life and thought in the twentieth century; **c.** the Reform movement is made up of a variety of attitudes and ideas, which sometimes conflict with one another; **d.** Jewish unity has been a goal far less important to major Reform leaders in the twentieth century than it was in the nineteenth century.

Here are some ideas that have been important to Reform Judaism over the years—but the words are all mixed up. Unscramble the words within the circles on the lines alongside. And remember: the Reform movement contains a number of conflicting ideas, and has undergone a variety of changes over the years; therefore, an idea in one circle may well oppose an idea in another circle.

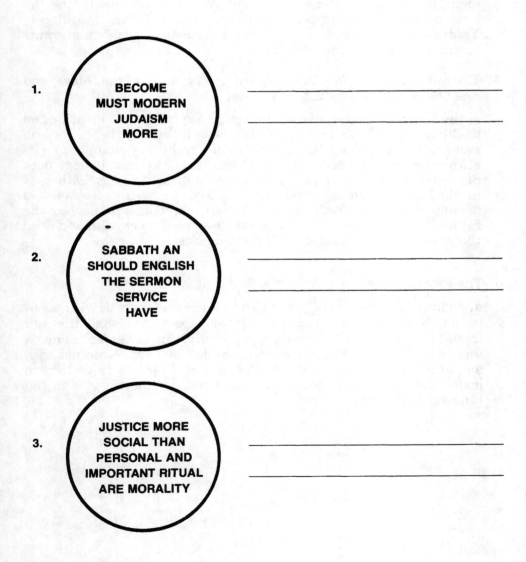

1.

BECOME
MUST MODERN
JUDAISM
MORE

_____

_____

2.

SABBATH AN
SHOULD ENGLISH
THE SERMON
SERVICE
HAVE

_____

_____

3.

JUSTICE MORE
SOCIAL THAN
PERSONAL AND
IMPORTANT RITUAL
ARE MORALITY

_____

_____

4.

STRIVE FOR
PEOPLE THE
UNITY JEWISH
MUST

_____
_____

5.

PEOPLE
NATION A THE
ARE JEWISH A
COMMUNITY BUT
RELIGIOUS NOT

_____
_____

6.

SHOULD
LANGUAGE
TO A JEWS
HAVE UNDERSTAND
NOT
THEY IN DON'T
PRAY

_____
_____

7.

CENTER LIFE
HOME OF AN
IMPORTANT IS
JEWISH THE

_____
_____

8.

DESERVE MEN
STATUS WOMEN
JEWISH EQUAL
WITH

_____

_____

9.

CHANGE MUST
OPEN JUDAISM
BE TO

_____

_____

10.

ISRAEL FOR
HOMELAND ALL
A IS JEWS
SPIRITUAL

_____

_____

THE REASONS WHY

In your own words, complete each of the following.

1. The United States was a particularly good setting for the Reform movement to take root and grow because

2. Nineteenth century American Reform leaders generally rejected the idea of Israel as a Jewish homeland because

3. Both Isaac Mayer Wise and Stephen S. Wise worked to create rabbinical seminaries because

4. The modern Reform movement has returned to many of the basics of Jewish tradition, such as ritual observance, home prayer, and the Hebrew language because

5. Reform Judaism arose in Europe, after the Jews were granted political freedom and economic opportunities because

6. Involvement with, and commitment to the state of Israel is a major element of Reform Judaism today because

Match each of the imaginary "speeches" in the right column below with the event or personality in the left column to which it refers. To indicate your choice, place the number before the particular event or personality in the blank space next to its matching speech.

1. Rabbi Stephen S. Wise

☐ "You are few in number, but far-reaching in your importance to American Jewish life. Not just because you are first, but because you are of this country, of this experience, and you will be able to relate to your future congregants as fellow Americans—not as spiritual ambassadors from Europe."

2. The Centenary Perspective

☐ "This man can truly be called a prophet, an individual dramatically ahead of his time— because he saw the shape of the future so clearly. He understood the power and passion of the eastern European Jewish immigrants, and worked hard to create a relationship with them. And as for Zionism and Israel, he brought us right back on track, right where we have always belonged."

3. Rabbi Isaac Mayer Wise

☐ "With this program, we move, at long last, into the nineteenth century. It's about time, I say! Let's be done, once and for all, with primitive superstition and meaningless rituals! Let us abandon, finally, the idea of nationhood—which is narrow and limiting—and concentrate, instead, upon our moral mission to all of humanity!"

4. The founding of the Hebrew Union College

☐ "The beauty of this work is that it brings us back to basics. Moreover it helps us to preserve our past and cherish our traditions—in the universal language of the Jewish people. And let's face it: it gives us the opportunity to correct an error that we made in years past."

5. The Pittsburgh Platform

☐ "The achievements of this man? It's like an endless numbers game—one doesn't know where to begin and where to end. The congregations. The school. The rabbinical association. His version of a united American Jewry has not yet come to pass, and may never do so, but it is a worthy aim, grand and sweeping in scope—so like the man himself!"

6. Publication of *The Gates of Prayer*

☐ "It is singularly fitting that our belief in, and commitment to the future might begin with a proud affirmation of our past. Who we are rests firmly and forever upon the foundation of who we have been, and what we have done. There is our history, our tradition, our ties with world Jewry, and, above all, our deep and powerful involvement with the Jewish state. We cannot overstate, on this landmark anniversary, the dangers confronting us today, in the aftermath of the Yom Kippur War—Arab oil, Israel's growing isolation, the promotion of the P.L.O. by various Third World countries, Soviet moves in the area—but neither should we ignore the challenges and opportunities."

Take a tour through the photographs that appear on pages 71-76. Examine them, and their accompanying captions for content and meaning. In the space below, is a set of features, attitudes, and values that can be found in Reform Judaism. Circle the number before the statement that is not expressed in the photographs.

1. Teaching morals and ethics to young people.

2. Creating a Jewish social atmosphere.

3. Involvement with social and political issues in the general community.

4. Making young people aware of Jewish history.

5. Striking a delicate balance between the old and the new.

6. Remembering the Holocaust.

7. Helping the Jewish elderly and poor.

8. Creating Jewish educational programs in an informal setting.

9. Sponsoring rallies for Soviet Jewry.

10. Creating new traditions.

REDISCOVERING TRADITION

Twentieth century Reform Judaism has been engaged in rediscovering important parts of tradition—the variety of festivals, rituals, ceremonies, attitudes, and practices that were cast away by an earlier generation—and in discovering why they are important.

The cycle of Jewish life below contains a number of traditions that Jews have cherished and sustained for centuries. In the space next to each tradition, try to explain its importance.

PRAYING IN HEBREW	**LIGHTING THE SABBATH CANDLES**
OBSERVING THE HIGH HOLY DAYS	**HAVING A PASSOVER SEDER**
READING THE TORAH ON THE SABBATH	**VISITING ISRAEL**
SAYING KADDISH FOR A DEAD PARENT	**CELEBRATING HANUKKAH**

THEN AND TODAY

List-making is a popular activity today. Let us see what we can learn about ourselves by making lists.

List #1: OUTSIDE INFLUENCES

The history of the Reform movement offers dramatic proof that Judaism has been deeply affected by outside influences, attitudes, and events in the world at large. Make a list of the outside influences—good and bad—that you think have helped shape and direct Jewish life today.

_____

_____

_____

_____

_____

_____

_____

_____

_____

_____

_____

_____

List #2: MAKING CHANGES

Reform Judaism has shown a remarkable ability to recognize and adapt to change, and to create a few changes of its own along the way. Are there major changes that you would like to make in Jewish life today? Write them down, and in each case briefly explain why. (You may think of more or less than four changes. List at least three.)

CHANGE | REASON

1. _____ | _____
   _____ | _____
   | _____
   | _____

2. _____ | _____
   _____ | _____
   | _____
   | _____

3. _____ | _____
   _____ | _____
   | _____
   | _____

4. _____ | _____
   _____ | _____
   | _____
   | _____

OTHERS

_____

_____

_____

_____

_____

The modern Reform movement places a good deal of emphasis upon the home as a vital center of Jewish life. How would you go about creating a Jewish home? The building blocks below represent a foundation for a strong Jewish home environment—depending upon the ingredients (experiences, values, customs, general lifestyle) that you decide to pour inside. Fill each building block with one such ingredient, and see what kind of Jewish home you would build.

REFORM JUDAISM: BELIEFS AND PRACTICES

5

TRUE OR FALSE*

1. Modern Reform Judaism places far more value upon ancient times and traditions than did the Reform movement of the nineteenth century?   **T   F**

2. Religious arts and crafts is one area of Jewish life in which the past has inspired the present?   **T   F**

3. Reform thinkers today believe that it is not God who has created human beings, but human beings who have created God—as a symbol of all that is good and true in the world?   **T   F**

4. In the twentieth century, the Reform movement embraced Zionism, among other reasons, because of certain attitudes and events in the outside world?   **T   F**

5. Now that Reform Judaism has moved closer to rituals, Zionism, and Hebrew, it has lost much of its passion for political consciousness and social justice?   **T   F**

6. Many Reform Jews call their synagogues "temples" as a symbol of solidarity with the ancient past, and as an expression of the hope that the holy temple will one day be rebuilt in Jerusalem?   **T   F**

7. Anti-Zionists, such as Isaac Mayer Wise, claimed that working for a homeland would involve Jews in politics and practical issues, and would distract them from their spiritual mission?   **T   F**

8. Modern Reform rabbis approve of intermarriage on two grounds: (i) love is more important than all other responsibilities; (ii) there is no surer way of moving Jews into the mainstream of American life?   **T   F**

9. The Reform movement has dropped the second day of many of the holy festivals, because that is the way it was done in the Bible?   **T   F**

10. Because of their concern for social action, Reform rabbis and lay leaders have been particularly involved in such causes as civil rights, decent working conditions, and the anti-war movement?   **T   F**

11. The Columbus Platform of 1937 declared that Reform Judaism, in its abandonment of rituals and mitzvot, had turned away from God's revealed Law?   **T   F**

12. In such spheres as working for Israel, raising money for various Jewish philanthropies, and helping persecuted Jewish communities, there is little difference between the efforts of Reform Jews and those of Orthodox, Conservative, Reconstructionist, and secular Jews?   **T   F**

ODD IDEA OUT*

Each of the statements below contains several sections, one of which is an "odd idea out." It is simply not true. Circle the letter before the section that should not be there.

1. In Reform Jewish thinking, God

    a. plays an active role in Jewish history; **b.** is defined and interpreted in a variety of ways; **c.** is an idea which includes, among other things, personal morality, and ideas of order and logic in the universe; **d.** is considered a factor that can divide and weaken the Jewish people.

2. On the question of Zionism and Israel, Classical Reform Jews

    a. rejected the idea of a Jewish nation; **b.** worried that their loyalty to America might be questioned if they supported these ideas; **c.** insisted that the creation of a Jewish state violated the idea of the coming of the Messiah, who would one day redeem the Jewish people and bring them back to their ancient homeland; **d.** declared that involvement with national hopes and aspirations would undermine Jewish spirituality.

3. Classical Reform Judaism

    a. rejected the ghetto, and yearned to be accepted by the surrounding, non-Jewish society; **b.** did not accept the Torah; **c.** did not believe that the Jews were a "Chosen People"; **d.** insisted that scattering Jews among the many nations was spiritually desirable to fulfill the Jewish Mission throughout the world.

4. In the area of religious observance, Reform Judaism

    a. has fiercely resisted changes of attitudes over the years; **b.** has come to understand that there are certain rituals and ceremonies that have to be observed properly to preserve the Jewish tradition; **c.** now believes that the observance of certain mitzvot can be an important part of a good Jewish life; **d.** has begun to move in the direction of formulating guidelines to ritual observance.

5. The Columbus Platform of 1937

    a. declared that a number of rituals must be considered valued elements of Judaism; **b.** proclaimed the importance of Hebrew in prayer and study; **c.** helped enlarge and intensify Jewish education within the Reform movement; **d.** made little impact upon many rabbis and lay leaders of the time.

WORD SCRAMBLE*

Each of the scrambled words below is an important element of Reform Judaism. Unscramble them. Place the correct words in the boxes that follow. Then unscramble the circled letters to reveal one of the Reform movement's major values. The circled letters in Column A make up the first word; those in Column B, the second word.

COLUMN A

1. **A T U Y B E**

2. **L A I R Y M O T**

3. **P A T T I R I S Y L I U**

4. **T R I V Y C A I T E**

COLUMN B

1. **T I U S C E J**

2. **T R E Y N O M I D**

3. **M O I N T U C Y M**

4. **A I L Q U Y T E**

5. **B I L E I X Y F L I T**

6. **A C T U N E I D O**

50

A SYNAGOGUE CALENDAR

SPECIAL PROJECT

Rabbi Eugene B. Borowitz believes that the truest idea of God will inspire us to keep Torah in our lives and preserve the Jewish people. The calendar of your synagogue is probably packed with a variety of activities—social, educational, ritual, community service, and ties with Israel. Choose the activities that, in your view, most effectively "keep Torah in our lives and preserve the Jewish people." Set them down in the synagogue calendar below—about three to five activities in each category—and assign them an order of importance.

SYNAGOGUE CALENDAR

"KEEP THE TORAH IN OUR LIVES"	"PRESERVE THE JEWISH PEOPLE"
1.	
2.	
3.	
4.	
5.	

CONFRONTATION

Imagine that you are the rabbi of a Modern Reform congregation, and are confronted by a Classical Reform Jew, who, by some miracle, has traveled through time from the nineteenth century. He is shocked by what he sees—as shocked, say, as an Orthodox Jew from eastern Europe might be to have visited *his* temple, Sunday morning service and all. He bombards you with angry statements and questions. How would you answer each of the following challenges?

1. "You have positively gone primitive! Pure oriental! The ceremonies and rituals that we threw out—with courage and vision, if I say so myself—you have brought right back in again! Why? Toward what end?"

2. "Do you know that you have members who seriously see God as a kind of supernatural miracle worker? Who talk about the parting of the Sea of Reeds, and making the sun stand still, and the creation of the world in six days! I mean really! You are supposed to be a citizen of the twentieth century! In my day—a hundred years ago—we were a lot more sophisticated than that. And you call yourselves Modern Reform! What you really are is superstitious!"

3. "Your idea of being an involved, committed Jew is to put the past on a pedestal, and pay special attention to it simply because it is the past. I reject this approach entirely. To me, what is most important is the present. And the future."

4. "You are sliding right back to the "Chosen People" business. Just like you did with the Bar Mitzvah custom. (I mean, can you honestly call a thirteen-year-old boy a man?) Can't you understand that the "Chosen People" concept is nothing but a way we have of patting ourselves on the back, which has gotten our people into no end of troubles over the centuries. Our belief in Israel's Mission, on the other hand, is universal in character; we are concerned not just with Jews, but with the moral well-being of all peoples."

5. "Okay. I grant you much has happened in this century to justify the creation of a Jewish state. But I still remain fundamentally opposed to it, and to the Zionist Movement in general. And once you become political, with all the wheeling and dealing and power that goes along with it, you lose your claim to spiritual purity. And that, to me, is what Judaism should really be about!"

PLATFORM BUILDING*

The Pittsburgh and Columbus Platforms were statements of principles, basic guidelines for a good Jewish life, as set down by Reform leaders of two very different eras. Up to now, we have studied attitudes and beliefs of Orthodox and Reform Judaism, and each of these groups is split into two smaller groupings: modern or liberal Orthodox and ultra-Orthodox; and Classical Reform and Modern Reform.

Below are "planks" from four different platforms—imaginary, of course. In the space provided in each plank assign it to the group (or groups) which might have written it. Use an **M** for Modern Reform, a **C** for Classical Reform, an **O** for liberal Orthodox, and a **U** for ultra-Orthodox.

Note: A plank may belong to more than one group; it may even belong to all four. Sometimes it belongs to an "odd couple"—two groups that seem very far apart. For example, one of the planks below could be part of an ultra-Orthodox *and* a Classical Reform position. When you make your choice, give a brief reason for it.

Plank #1

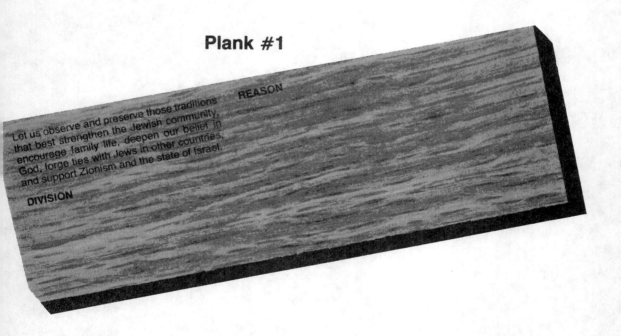

REASON

Let us observe and preserve those traditions that best strengthen the Jewish community, encourage family life, deepen our belief in God, forge ties with Jews in other countries, and support Zionism and the state of Israel.

DIVISION

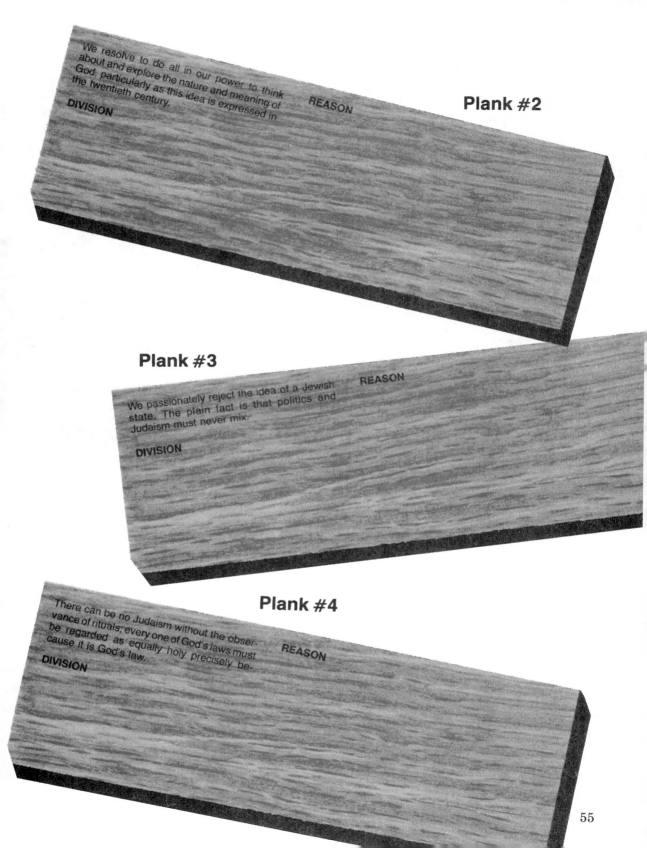

Plank #2

We resolve to do all in our power to think about and explore the nature and meaning of God, particularly as this idea is expressed in the twentieth century.

REASON

DIVISION

Plank #3

We passionately reject the idea of a Jewish state. The plain fact is that politics and Judaism must never mix.

REASON

DIVISION

Plank #4

There can be no Judaism without the observance of rituals; every one of God's laws must be regarded as equally holy precisely because it is God's law.

REASON

DIVISION

55

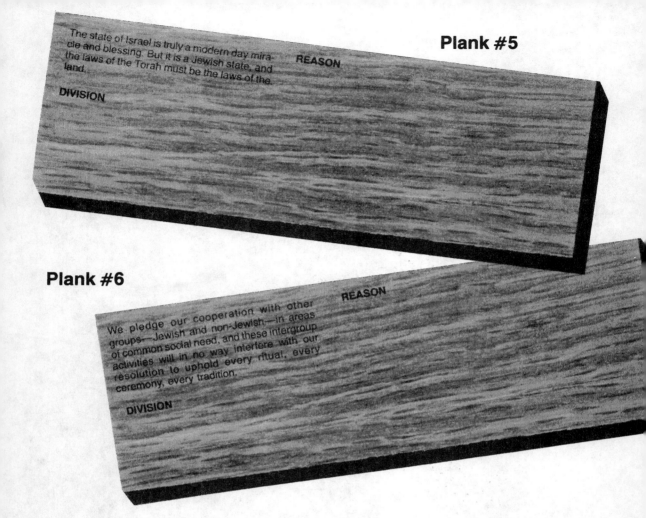

Plank #5

The state of Israel is truly a modern day miracle and blessing. But it is a Jewish state, and the laws of the Torah must be the laws of the land.

REASON

DIVISION

Plank #6

We pledge our cooperation with other groups—Jewish and non-Jewish—in areas of common social need, and these intergroup activities will in no way interfere with our resolution to uphold every ritual, every ceremony, every tradition.

REASON

DIVISION

Plank #7

We will do all in our power to relieve the suffering of oppressed Jewish communities wherever they might be.

REASON

DIVISION

Plank #8

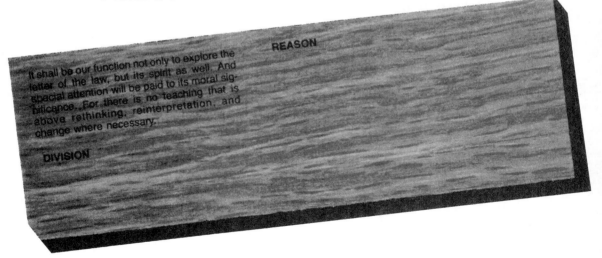

REASON

It shall be our function not only to explore the letter of the law, but its spirit as well. And special attention will be paid to its moral significance. For there is no teaching that is above rethinking, reinterpretation, and change where necessary.

DIVISION

SOCIAL JUSTICE AND PERSONAL MORALITY

1. Profile of a Problem

Reform Judaism has always stressed the ideals of social justice and personal morality. Choose what you believe to be the most glaring, outrageous example of social injustice within your own community, and do a profile of it by answering the following questions.

ISSUE

a. Briefly describe the social injustice.

_____

_____

_____

b. What are its causes? (There are usually more than one.)

_____

_____

_____

c. What are its major consequences? (For example, a consequence of extreme poverty might be a dramatic rise in crime.)

_____

_____

_____

d. What do you think are the main obstacles to its solution?

_____

_____

_____

2. A Blueprint For Social Change

Social injustice is usually deep-rooted and complex; it is not about to be wished away by an earnest smile or a noble statement. There is usually a long messy step-by-step process involved, with lots of hard work and more than a little pain along the way. Take the social injustice that you discussed above and, in the blueprint below, work out a step-by-step approach to its solution. If you think that this particular injustice cannot be solved, state the reasons for your opinion. In the space marked "can be solved," briefly set forth those elements that, in your opinion, spell the end of this particular social injustice. For example, if the problem were abuse of the elderly, the elements of solution might include financial security, easily available medical facilities, and acceptance and understanding by family and community.

PROBLEM

_____

STEP #1

_____

STEP #2

_____

STEP #3

_____

STEP #4

_____

CAN BE SOLVED ☐   CANNOT BE SOLVED ☐

Reasons

CONSERVATIVE JUDAISM: TRADITION AND CHANGE

6

ACHIEVEMENTS AND AWARDS*

The history of Conservative Judaism is graced with a remarkable cast of individuals, who played major roles in its growth and development. Each of the imaginary awards below describes the achievements of one of these individuals. In the blank write in the name of the person to whom that particular award would be given.

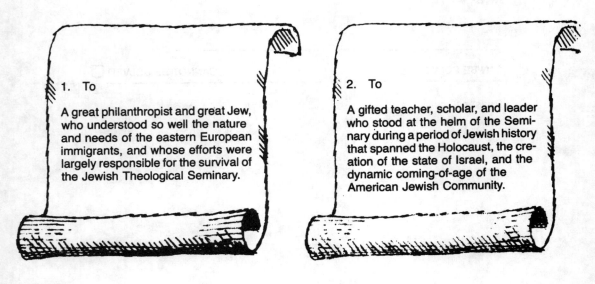

1. To

A great philanthropist and great Jew, who understood so well the nature and needs of the eastern European immigrants, and whose efforts were largely responsible for the survival of the Jewish Theological Seminary.

2. To

A gifted teacher, scholar, and leader who stood at the helm of the Seminary during a period of Jewish history that spanned the Holocaust, the creation of the state of Israel, and the dynamic coming-of-age of the American Jewish Community.

3. To

A pioneer whose vision was truly prophetic and would have taken root and flourished in a different time and place. The institution that he founded was a forerunner of the Jewish Theological Seminary in this country. And his approach to Judaism is the intellectual foundation of the Conservative movement today.

4. To

A scholar of international fame, an educator of genius, and an organizer of uncommon talent and daring, who, more than anyone else, can be called the architect of the Jewish Theological Seminary, and a great guiding spirit of the Conservative movement in the early years of this century.

5. To

A person of so many accomplishments, one doesn't know where to begin. Rabbi, educator, writer, editor, translator, founder of a rabbinical school—a traditional Jew in the deepest sense, who passionately believed in changes when necessary. He struck a delicate balance between Orthodox and Reform at a time when middle of the road moderation was a painfully lonely, and frequently misunderstood, position. A striking model for the Conservative rabbis who came after him.

6. To

A magnificent gambler who was present at the creation, not of one rabbinical institution but of two. Who had the wisdom to withdraw from one venture when he saw where it was going, and the courage to begin another. With few students, fewer resources, and great distances to travel, he assumed leadership at an age when most men are preparing to retire. And he died without ever knowing whether or not the Seminary would, or could, survive. His work in this area must be called a great act of faith.

HISTORICAL LESSONS*

The statements below contain a number of historical lessons drawn directly from the text. In each statement, however, there is one section that is an "outsider"—it is false. Circle the letter before the section that does not belong.

1. The various photographs, (on pages 93, 95, 99, 100, 101, 102, 103, 104) and accompanying captions teach that

    a. rigorous, systematic study of our history, culture, and tradition is an important element of Conservative Judaism; **b.** in terms of daily ritual, observant Conservative Jews strongly resemble modern Reform Jews; **c.** education is available at various levels to all who want it; it is a process that can begin in early childhood and continue throughout a person's life; **d.** Conservative Judaism is sometimes caught between two conflicting values: the need to preserve tradition, and the need to change.

2. A review of Solomon Schechter's career at the Jewish Theological Seminary teaches that

    a. the way in which its clergy is educated can help shape and direct a religious movement; **b.** the knowledge and understanding of traditional Jewish sources was considered an aim of high priority in the Conservative movement—an aim to be actively pursued; **c.** the view and policy of the Seminary was that faith, independent intellectual inquiry, and the right to speak freely always conflict with one another; **d.** a great institution of higher learning is made up of a number of important parts, and is usually the product of a step-by-step process.

3. The creation of the Rabbinical Assembly of America in 1919 teaches that

    a. the Conservative movement understood that its ideas and values would be strengthened by a solid organizational structure; **b.** Conservative Judaism recognized the importance of granting their rabbis professional status, and relating to them in a professional way; **c.** being part of a national organization helped Conservative rabbis to become better scholars and educators; **d.** the various parts of the Conservative movement go their own separate ways and have little to do with one another.

4. Isaac Leeser's work teaches that

a. it is important that Jews understand the meaning of their prayers and studies; b. nineteenth century Jewish leaders in this country were seeking some kind of spiritual middle ground between Orthodox and Reform Judaism; c. Conservative leaders were among the earliest opponents of Jewish settlement in Israel; d. a movement, religious or political, can sometimes be set into motion by the work, energy, and personal example of a single individual.

5. The efforts of Sabato Morais, Cyrus Adler and Jacob Schiff, and Alexander Kohut teach that

a. American Jewish leaders welcomed the effects of the Reform movement upon Judaism in this country; b. in its early stages, American Conservative Judaism faced a lonely, uphill struggle, with no assurance of success; c. the very term "Conservative" with its double meaning, helped the young movement to better define its aims, and to create a set of clear standards and guidelines; d. a number of American Reform Jews of German ancestry proved to be sensitive and responsive to the needs of recently arrived eastern European Jewish immigrants.

6. The purposes set forth by the United Synagogue of America in 1913 teach that

a. the Conservative movement views Judaism as being part of a dynamic, continuing historical process; b. Conservative Judaism is deeply committed to preserving all of Jewish tradition, no matter what; c. Zionism has always been a cherished major value of Conservative Judaism; d. the Hebrew language has always been a key element in Conservative Jewish life.

A CYCLE OF CONSERVATIVE JEWISH LIFE*

Conservative Judaism is made up of many organizational parts serving a variety of purposes. Each section of the circle below describes a particular purpose. In the space above the section, write in the organizational part to which it refers.

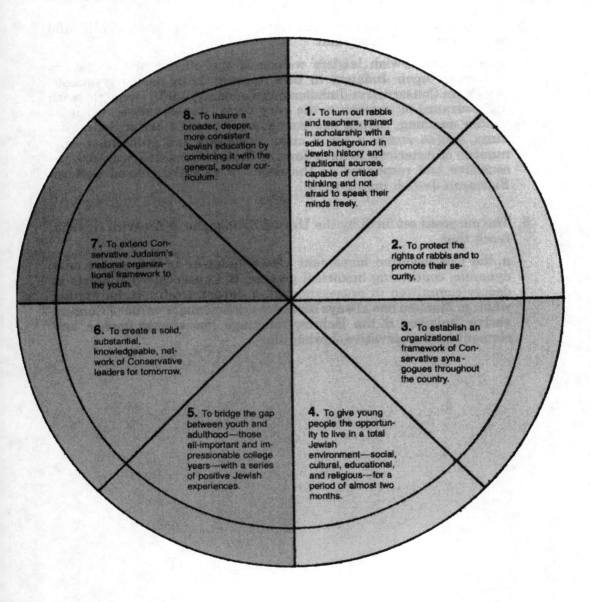

8. To insure a broader, deeper, more consistent Jewish education by combining it with the general, secular curriculum.

1. To turn out rabbis and teachers, trained in scholarship with a solid background in Jewish history and traditional sources, capable of critical thinking and not afraid to speak their minds freely.

7. To extend Conservative Judaism's national organizational framework to the youth.

2. To protect the rights of rabbis and to promote their security.

6. To create a solid, substantial, knowledgeable, network of Conservative leaders for tomorrow.

3. To establish an organizational framework of Conservative synagogues throughout the country.

5. To bridge the gap between youth and adulthood—those all-important and impressionable college years—with a series of positive Jewish experiences.

4. To give young people the opportunity to live in a total Jewish environment—social, cultural, educational, and religious—for a period of almost two months.

64

INSIGHTS IN DEPTH

Support each of the following statements with a brief reference to, or quotation from, the text (including the photographs and captions in the chapter and those in the special section beginning on page 99). In most instances, there are several supporting references or quotations; any one will do.

1. Conservative Judaism has always had a close, creative relationship with the state of Israel.

   _____

   _____

   _____

   _____

2. Conservative religious practice can be described as a process of preserving old traditions, while remaining open to new ideas.

   _____

   _____

   _____

   _____

3. The Conservative movement places great value upon Jewish scholarship.

   _____

   _____

   _____

   _____

4. Conservative Judaism has used a variety of approaches to educate its young people.

   _____

   _____

   _____

   _____

5. While open to change, Conservative leaders have considered the preservation of tradition a matter of the highest principle and priority.

_____

_____

_____

_____

6. The United States has proved to be a particularly favorable environment for the growth and development of Conservative Judaism.

_____

_____

_____

_____

IMAGINARY SERMONS*

Match the imaginary sermon in the right column with the event to which it refers to in the left column. Place the number before the event in the blank before the matching sermon.

1. The decision of Conservative leaders *not* to work within the Reform movement.

☐ "This is our history, our law, the record of everything we have been. It is meant to be read and discussed and thought about and loved. The aim of this project is not to ignore a Jewish language; it is to educate the Jewish people."

2. The opening of the first Ramah Camp.

☐ "Here we have the concept of Klal Yisrael—the world Jewish community—in action. Congregations from so many different lands have come together, joined hands, and made a moving expression of common belonging and shared belief."

3. Isaac Leeser's translation of the Bible into English.

☐ "It has been said that the soul of a people dwells in its schools. This school is the first of its kind in the United States. Its graduates can best serve the generations of our children and their children by teaching our tradition. To preserve is to renew."

4. The dedication of the Yeshurun Synagogue.

☐ "The fact is, living in the Diaspora as we do, our Judaism is conducted on a part-time basis. But here, our sons and daughters will know what it's like to live Jewishly twenty-four hours a day, every day."

5. The opening of the Jewish Theological Ceremony.

☐ "Yes, the unity of the Jewish people is a value of great importance. But unity at what price? A violation of our laws? A casting away of our traditions? A denial of our nationhood? A rejection of our homeland, of our Sabbath, of our holy language—of who we are, and what we stand for?"

6. The establishment of the World Council of Synagogues.

☐ "To quote the prophet, Isaiah, 'From out of Zion will the law go forth. And the word of the Lord from Jerusalem!' On this day, we have taken a page from the story of the Zionist pioneers, and proclaimed our ties with the land of Israel by taking part in the creation of this holy institution. We have struck roots in the city of Jerusalem!"

THE MAKING OF A MODERN JEW

Solomon Schechter's achievements as president of the Jewish Theological Seminary show the value of a carefully thought out, step-by-step approach to a goal. A wisely chosen faculty, a substantial library, the Hebrew Teacher's Institute, rigorous educational standards, a broad base of knowledge, coupled with the tradition of independent thought and free expression, were all elements that went into making the Seminary what it is today.

How about the making of a modern Jew? Which elements would you want to pour into that creation? Imagine that you are a few years older, and about to begin the process of raising your own child. You want him or her to be many things, among others a good Jew. Well, good Jews, like good schools, do not spring out of nowhere. They are the products of careful planning and hard work. What kind of Jew would you want your child to be, in terms of knowledge, beliefs, lifestyle, activities, and values?

1. Definition

Complete the following sentence: *I would like my child, as a good Jew, to*

2. Establishing Priorities

The qualities and characteristics below are all elements associated with being a good Jew. Rate them in what you believe to be their order of importance.

_____ Strict Sabbath observance

_____ A firm belief in God

_____ Personal sensitivity and compassion

_____ A sense of involvement with Jews from other lands

_____ A strong sense of social justice

_____ Active membership in a synagogue

_____ Conscientious keeping of the mitzvot

_____ A wide knowledge of Jewish history and tradition.

_____ Love of, and identification with, the state of Israel

_____ A strong Jewish atmosphere at home

CONSERVATIVE JUDAISM: BELIEFS AND PRACTICES

7

TRUE OR FALSE*

1. Conservative Jews have a variety of different ideas about the nature and meaning of God.   **T F**

2. The Conservative movement is far less defined by a single ideology than are the Orthodox and Reform movements.   **T F**

3. Although Conservative Judaism contains many different viewpoints, its various congregations observe exactly the same rituals on the Sabbath and holy days.   **T F**

4. Conservative Judaism places great emphasis and value upon the study of Jewish history and tradition.   **T F**

5. Because it has been so busy building its congregations, reinterpreting the law, educating its youth, promoting a positive sense of Jewish identity, and forging strong ties with Israel and world Jewry, Conservative leaders have been forced to ignore most issues of social justice within the general non-Jewish community. **T F**

6. In Conservative thought, the single most important measure of being a good Jew is consistent, unquestioning observance of our ritual laws. **T F**

7. A number of Conservative Jewish leaders have changed their opinions of separation of religion and state because of the growing financial need of Jewish Day Schools. **T F**

8. There has been a loss of support for Israel among American Conservative Jews because of the Orthodox control of religious life in the Jewish state. **T F**

9. The Conservative movement supports the position that prayers may be modernized both in terms of substance and style. **T F**

10. Conservative leaders generally agree that Israel offers a far greater opportunity to live a fulfilling Jewish life than any community in the Diaspora. **T F**

MYSTERY EDITORIALS*

THEN & TODAY

The following imaginary editorials come from either Orthodox, Conservative, or Reform journals. In the space after each excerpt, tell who wrote it (**O** for Orthodox; **C** for Conservative; and—you guessed it!—**R** for Reform), briefly state the reason for your choice. And remember, each group embraces a wide range of opinion—Classical and Modern Reform; liberal and ultra-Orthodox; Conservative that veers to the Orthodox, and Conservative that veers to the Reform. Therefore, the R in one statement might signify a Classical Reform view, while the R in a second statement might signify a Modern Reform view.

1. "We are not a chosen people! We are a people with a Mission—charged with a moral message that has to be spread around the world!"

☐

REASON: _____

_____

_____

_____

_____

2. "*November 1862*. The Jewish colonists in Palestine need our support, and we give it freely, generously, and without hesitation! This is an expression of Klal Yisrael, a value every bit as important as prayer and study!"

☐

REASON: _____

_____

_____

_____

_____

3. "Tradition and change do not conflict with one another; they actually go hand-in-hand."

☐

REASON: _____

_____

_____

_____

_____

4. "The Land of Israel—yes! The state of Israel—never! As for the return of the Jewish people to its ancient homeland, that must wait for the coming of the Messiah!"

☐

REASON: _____

_____

_____

_____

_____

_____

5. "Saturday or Sunday—what's the difference? The main thing is that we come together and pray to God. Those who oppose us are so concerned with what we did in the past that they ignore the needs of today."

☐

REASON: _____

_____

_____

_____

_____

6. "The line of distinction that these so-called modern Jews draw is false and misleading. There is no such thing as laws that are more important, and laws that are less important. Ritual laws and ethical laws are of equal value, because they have both been revealed to us by God!"

☐

REASON: _____

_____

_____

_____

_____

7. "It is not true that we will not cooperate with other Jewish groups. There are issues of mutual interest—support of Israel, working to relieve the plight of persecuted Jews abroad, helping the Jewish elderly and poor in this country—where we can and should pool our resources and efforts. But we must draw the line on questions of Jewish law and ritual observance. In this area, there can be no dialogue, no compromise. These are our principles, our sacred beliefs."

☐

REASON: _____

_____

_____

_____

_____

8. "There is no argument. We *do* bend the law a bit. But any changes that we make (which come about only after a good deal of painful soul-searching on our part) are based on logic and compassion. If the synagogue is miles away from a person's home, riding is far more sensible than, say, exhausting yourself, possibly endangering your health, or not coming to services at all. On the other hand, using the car to travel to the beach or to a ball game, we too reject. That is a clear-cut violation of the spirit of the Sabbath."

☐

REASON: _____

_____

_____

_____

_____

9. "Of course tradition has an important place in our scheme of things. Tradition is educational; people can relate to a concrete ritual a lot more easily than they can to an abstract idea. And regular observance of certain ceremonies gives a person emotional ties to his or her religion, which are so very important, as well as bonds with other Jews who do the same thing. What lovelier sight is there than children watching their mother light the Sabbath candles? However, it is not for us to say 'Thou shalt do this' and 'Thou shalt not do that.' Ritual observance is strictly a matter of individual decision."

☐

REASON: _____

_____

_____

_____

_____

_____

10. "We are part of, not apart from, a continuing historical process. We move, we grow, we change. To admit this does not negate our tradition; rather, it gives it new possibilities. And it brings *us* into the picture, engages *us* in a spiritual dialogue, gives *us* the opportunity to inquire, to analyze, to interpret, and to discover."

☐

REASON: _____

_____

_____

_____

_____

LOOKING FOR UNDERSTANDING

SPECIAL FEATURE

The questions below offer crucial keys to understanding Conservative Judaism. Answer them briefly and clearly.

1. Anything new is usually a response to an existing need. Conservative Judaism is a new movement that has taken root and flourished. What need, or needs, of the Jewish people has it answered?

_____

_____

_____

_____

_____

2. To borrow a thought from Solomon Schechter, why can a religious movement *not* survive on high minded ideas alone? What else does it need?

_____

_____

_____

_____

_____

3. What do you think that Professor Heschel meant by his statement, "Israel is a holy people whose task is to prove that in order to be a people, we have to be more than a people"?

_____

_____

_____

_____

4. How would you define Klal Yisrael? Can you give an example of this idea in action in our own time?

_____

_____

_____

_____

5. How do you explain the statement: "Revelation is a two-way process, or a dialogue between God and humanity"?

_____

_____

_____

_____

And the statement: "The Bible and Jewish laws are our response to God's call; the mitzvah is human interpretation and application of Divine principles"?

_____

_____

_____

_____

How do these two statements support the idea of change, as it is expressed in Conservative thinking?

_____

_____

_____

_____

6. How would you explain the idea that Israel must be more than a state, that it must be a spiritual center for world Jewry?

_____

_____

_____

_____

Can you give an example of how Israel has fulfilled this obligation?

_____

_____

_____

_____

A LITTLE BIT OF THIS AND THAT

If you were a Conservative Jew, how would you answer the following challenge, which could come from an Orthodox Jew, a Reform Jew, or a non-Jew?

"The problem with your brand of Judaism is that it is really no brand at all; it is a hodge-podge of history and ritual that stands nowhere, and seems to be going nowhere. I mean, whether or not one likes Orthodoxy, it stands for something. So does Reform! There is something to hold onto, something to believe in or to reject. Conservative Judaism, on the other hand, seems to have settled in a spiritual no man's land, teetering on a tightrope of convenience and confusion. A little bit of this and that with no clear-cut definition, no binding direction, no real center of gravity!"

1. The Spirit of the Law

Conservative Judaism insists that every law, every custom, every ceremony, be open to independent inquiry. And in the process of exploration, it tries to draw a sharp, careful line of distinction between the letter of the law and its spirit—as was the case in its decision to allow riding to the synagogue on the Sabbath. After each of the rituals presented in the mosaic below, write in what you believe is the spirit of the law, or its underlying reason.

ISSUE

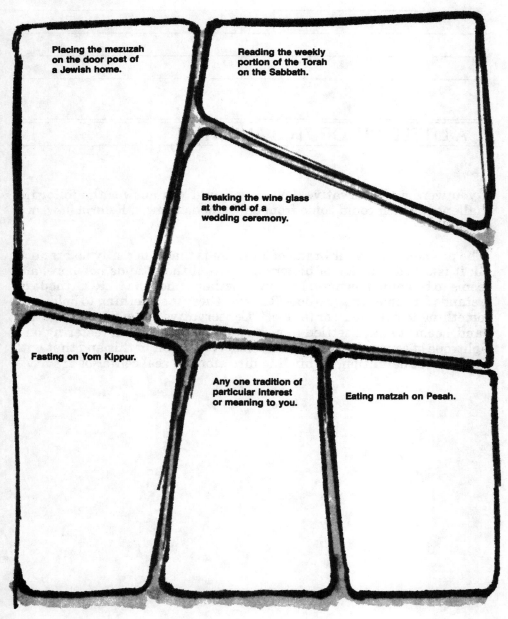

Placing the mezuzah on the door post of a Jewish home.

Reading the weekly portion of the Torah on the Sabbath.

Breaking the wine glass at the end of a wedding ceremony.

Fasting on Yom Kippur.

Any one tradition of particular interest or meaning to you.

Eating matzah on Pesah.

2. Forecasting the Future

Conservative thinkers believe that Judaism does not exist in a vacuum, but is part of a continuing, dynamic historical process. Do you see any event or development today that is likely to change Jewish life in the future? What is your choice, and why? And what kind of change do you think it may bring?

_____

_____

_____

_____

_____

_____

_____

_____

_____

_____

_____

_____

_____

_____

_____

_____

ODD IDEA OUT*

Each of the statements below contains several sections, one of which is an "odd idea out" because it contradicts the content or meaning of the material in the chapter. Circle the letter before the false section.

1. In Professor Louis Ginzberg's view, Jewish law

   a. can only be changed by a majority of the people; **b.** is what the Jewish religion is really about; **c.** is part of an active, continuing historical process; **d.** must be constantly and carefully explored, analyzed, reinterpreted, and adapted to a changing world.

2. On the question of interfaith activities:

   a. some Conservative leaders view them as a crucial means of conquering anti-Semitism, and of promoting communication and understanding between Jews and non-Jews; **b.** Conservative leaders insist, as a matter of policy, that all Orthodox and Reform Jews should assume equal authority and responsibility in this sphere; **c.** several Conservative leaders have already gone to great lengths to break down barriers, and build positive new relationships; **d.** a few Conservative leaders worry that some Christian spokesmen might use interfaith dialogue as instruments for criticizing Judaism and converting Jews.

3. The idea of Klal Yisrael

   a. has always been a central value of the Conservative movement; **b.** is the basis upon which the state of Israel has built its unique relationship with world Jewry; **c.** has been expressed by such projects as Youth Aliyah, the Law of the Return, rallies for oppressed Jewish communities, and the like; **d.** is so important to Conservative Judaism because that movement believes in the concept of the chosen people.

4. According to Rabbi Gordis,

   a. without a firm belief in revelation, Judaism would quickly disintegrate; **b.** Jewish life in the present is built upon Jewish life in the past; **c.** it is important that the Jewish people learn, and put into practice, good ethical and social values; **d.** Jewish tradition is not isolated, not locked away in a ghetto; it relates to everything in our lives—our culture, our society, the whole world.

5. In Conservative thinking, God

   a. is often associated with forces of goodness, progress, and creativity; **b.** is sometimes perceived as a power within people; **c.** may have but one meaning; **d.** is believed by some to be an all-knowing, all-powerful presence that fills the world.

6. The ideas of tradition and change

   a. express the Conservative view that rituals and ceremonies are valuable parts of Jewish life, and should be handled with extreme care; **b.** express the view that Jewish life is a part of a constantly moving historical process; **c.** make the point that Judaism is not just a creed, not just a body of belief, but a religious civilization; **d.** are the reasons for the differences between the various competing factions in the Conservative movement.

HIDDEN WORD HUNT*

In the maze of letters below are hidden eight words, including one two-word term, that are important elements in the Conservative movement's network of beliefs and practices. They may be written vertically, horizontally, diagonally, at the beginning of a line, or in the middle, and occasionally, may even be caught creeping around a corner. Two words may intersect and share a letter. As long as the letters are set down in some kind of consecutive order, one after the other, they are fine. When you have hunted down a hidden word, draw a circle around it.

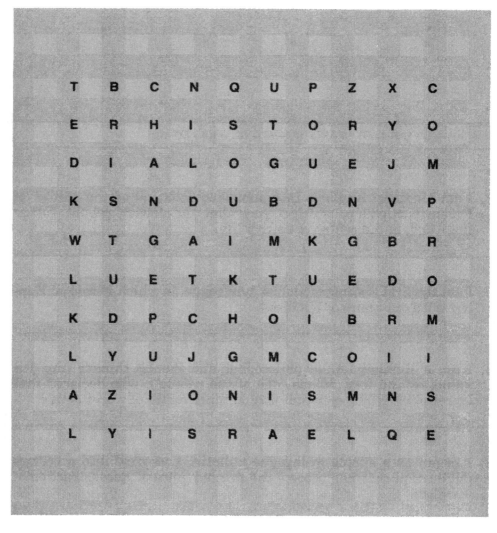

RECON-STRUCTIONIST JUDAISM FROM PHILOSOPHY TO MOVEMENT

8

WHO, WHAT, AND WHERE AM I?*

1. I am Mordecai Kaplan's first published book, called the "Bible" of Reconstructionism, which argues that the Jewish people, rather than God, is the center of Jewish life.

   _____

2. I am the first Reconstructionist synagogue, in which Mordecai Kaplan tried out many of his ideas.

   _____

3. I am a Russian-Jewish philosopher and Zionist thinker (my pen name, by the way, means "one of the people"), who declared that Israel must be the spiritual and cultural center of world Jewry.

   _____

4. I began as a simple synagogue bulletin, and grew into a serious publication that has become the printed voice of Reconstructionist Judaism.

   _____

5. I am the renowned Russian-Jewish historian, who argued that every Jewish community must develop into an independent, creative unit—a kind of small civilization in its own right.

_____

6. I am the religious volume, published at the end of World War II, which sparked arguments within the Jewish community and inspired many angry attacks upon Mordecai Kaplan, even from Conservative rabbis.

_____

7. I am the institution of higher learning, designed to train reconstructionist rabbis. Like Yeshivah University, the Jewish Theological Seminary, and the Hebrew Union College and the Jewish Institute of Religion, I am living proof that creating a rabbinical school is a most important step for any Jewish religious movement.

_____

8. My creation signified the break between Reconstructionism and Conservative and Reform Judaism, and the real beginning of an independent Reconstructionists movement. (I am known by a slightly different name today; either one will do).

_____

INSIGHTS IN DEPTH

Support each of the statements below with a reference to, or quotation from, the text—including the photographs and captions in the chapter and those in the special section of photos beginning on page 124.

1. Reconstructionist Judaism did not hesitate to change, and even transform, Jewish ritual and tradition.

_____

_____

_____

2. The Jewish Theological Seminary tries to stand behind members of its faculty who are nonconformists and even figures of controversy.

_____

_____

_____

_____

3. Zionism and Israel are not just two of many other values of Reconstructionism; they are the heart and soul of the movement.

_____

_____

_____

_____

4. Reconstructionist Judaism views ritual as a means to an end, rather than as an end in itself.

_____

_____

_____

_____

5. Reconstructionism has cut across the religious and political boundary lines of Jewish life to communicate its message and win members.

_____

_____

_____

_____

6. Reconstructionism is particularly well-suited to bridge the gap between generations.

_____

_____

_____

_____

7. Mordecai Kaplan was concerned with many conflicting values, views, and considerations.

_____

_____

_____

_____

8. An Orthodox Jew will reject the Jewish lifestyle of a Reconstructionist, even if the latter faithfully observes all of the mitzvot.

_____

_____

_____

_____

9. Kaplan, always the man of action as well as thought, saw organizational structure as the most effective means of bringing ideas into being and putting them to work.

_____

_____

_____

_____

VALUES AND VANTAGE POINTS*

A Reconstructionist might be every bit as observant as an Orthodox Jew, but would be doing it for different reasons. It is a question of vantage points. For example, an Orthodox Jew would read the Torah or keep the Sabbath simply because these are mitzvot, God's commands. A Reconstructionist Jew, on the other hand, might read the same Torah portion or keep the Sabbath with equal knowledge, understanding, and fervor, but he or she would be doing so for social, cultural, or moral reasons, or because these acts somehow strengthen the Jewish community.

This chapter has presented a broad picture of Reconstructionist philosophy. Read the excerpts below. Some of them do reflect Reconstructionist vantage points and values; others do not. In the space that follows each excerpt, write in "yes" if it reflects the Reconstructionist position or "no" if it does not, and then briefly explain why.

1. "What we have to say is for all Jews. We hope to establish a dialogue with Orthodox, Conservative, Reform, Zionist, and secular Jews alike. Belief must not become a barrier to contact and communication between Jews!" _____

_____

_____

_____

_____

2. "There are two aspects of the Kol Nidre Service on Yom Kippur Eve that particularly please me. First, there is the prayer itself, which goes back to the time of the Spanish Inquisition and the Marranos; this creates a bond of community between present and past. And second, the value of community and the idea of mutual responsibility are movingly expressed in the words: "for the sin that *we* have sinned!" _____

_____

_____

_____

_____

3. "What do I find most inspiring about the state of Israel? This might surprise you. Not its new communities such as the Kibbutz and the Moshav. Not the fact that it drained the swamps and made the desert bloom. Not technological achievements. And not even its military prowess, as heroic and miraculous as that has been. No, what really touches me is the Ingathering of the Exiles. And the Law of the Return, which is written into Israel's Declaration of Independence. And the work it has done with Soviet Jewry—sometimes at a high

social and political price to itself. And the *shlihim*, or emissaries, that it has sent to Jewish communities abroad. And how it helped Holocaust victims during and after World War II. That, to me, tells what Israel *really* is—and should be—about!" _____

_____

_____

_____

_____

4. "The fact is, Judaism is made up of many different elements—history, ethics, language, culture, folklore, ritual, ceremony, social movements—all of which have helped shape who we are today, and what we stand for. Now I grant you, religion has played a very important role in our development, but it is not everything, nor has it ever been. There is but one common denominator of the Jewish experience down through the ages, and that is the Jewish people. Judaism stands or falls with us—period!" _____

_____

_____

_____

_____

5. "If anything, the Torah is a great spiritual achievement precisely because it was written by people, rather than given by God. It is a creation of genius. But the fact is we change. Our society and culture changes. Why can't the laws governing our lives change, as well? We are called 'The People of the Book.' Well, is the 'Book' meant to be read, studied, thought about, and applied—or to be made a shrine, an untouchable idol to be paid homage and worshipped?" _____

_____

_____

_____

_____

6. "The fact is, there are large differences of culture and philosophy that cannot, and should not, be wished away. What does a Jew from Riga, Latvia, truly have in common with a Jew, say, from Atlanta, Georgia? Shouldn't differing backgrounds and divergent beliefs be respected? Maybe our differences are marks of identity and integrity that should be left strictly alone!" _____

_____

_____

_____

_____

7. "I agree. Hebrew is *Lashon Hakodesh*, the holy tongue. And what really makes it so is that it can be an instrument of communication, a source of unity, for Jews the world over." _____

_____

_____

_____

_____

8. "There are certain traditions and beliefs that are sacred. They have been with us for many centuries, and so must be accepted and cherished. They should not be tinkered or tampered with. Let us simply preserve them and enjoy them as they are. That is the meaning of faith!" _____

_____

_____

_____

_____

EVENTS AND EFFECTS*

Match the events in the left column with the changes that they helped bring about in the right column. Make your choice by placing the number before the event in the blank space before the matching effect.

1. The formation of the Fellowship of Reconstructionist Congregations (known today as the Federation of Reconstructionist Congregations and Fellowships).

   ☐ Gave the new movement a voice that could be "heard" around the country.

2. The publication of *Judaism as a Civilization*

   ☐ Made Mordecai Kaplan deeply, painfully aware that the Jewish people must inhabit two worlds that can, and often do, come into conflict with one another.

3. The creation of *The Reconstructionist Magazine*

   ☐ Underscored the idea that Israel must never become "a nation like all other nations." Defined Israel's unique role as the spiritual and cultural center of world Jewry.

4. Kaplan's experiences in Paris, and on the ship to America

   ☐ Provided a community in which Kaplan's Reconstructionist ideas could be put to work with people in practical day-to-day terms.

5. The writings of Ahad Ha-am

   ☐ Set forth, in depth and detail, the Reconstructionist philosophy and program; laid down lines of definition for those who embraced this brand of Judaism—and lines of opposition for those who were against it.

6. The establishment of the Society for the Advancement of Judaism

   ☐ Marked the beginning of Reconstructionist Judaism as an independent movement—the fourth major movement in modern Jewish life.

THE REASONS WHY

In your own words, complete each of the following.

1. Mordecai Kaplan's *Judaism as a Civilization* created an explosion in Jewish life and thought because

2. Kaplan and his followers believed it necessary to publish *The New Haggadah* and the *Sabbath Prayer Book* because

3. Zionism and Israel are central elements in the Reconstructionist philosophy because

4. For many years Kaplan refused to allow the Reconstructionist movement to break away from Conservative Jewry because

5. Although a thinker, scholar, and writer, Kaplan spent a good deal of his time and energy in organizational work because

6. Simon Dubnow and Ahad Ha-am had particularly strong influences upon Reconstructionist thinking because

7. Reconstructionism was able to cut across boundary lines of belonging and belief "to win followers among Conservative and Reform rabbis and laypeople as well as in Zionist and secularist ranks" because

8. Mordecai Kaplan finally agreed that Reconstructionist Judaism had to become a religious movement in its own right because

IDEA SCRAMBLE*

Here are some ideas that are important elements of Reconstructionist thinking—but the words are all mixed up. Unscramble the words within the various circles, and on the lines alongside, write down the ideas that each group expresses.

1. SPIRITUAL JEWRY THE OF

   ISRAEL IS CENTER WORLD

   _____

   _____

2. SOCIAL A IS RELIGION

   EXPERIENCE

   _____

   _____

3. UNIT THE LIFE COMMUNITY

   OF BASIC THE JEWISH IS

   _____

   _____

4. LIFE PARTICIPANTS BE WOMEN

   FULLY MUST JEWISH IN EQUAL

   _____

   _____

5. UNITY OF OBSERVANCE JEWISH

   SOURCE A RITUAL IS

   _____

   _____

6. CREATION THE PEOPLE OF

   TORAH IS THE

   _____

   _____

7. THOUGHTFUL TO OPEN BELIEFS

   BE EXAMINATION MUST

   _____

   _____

8. IMPORTANT IS PEOPLE CONCERN

   THE JUDAISM'S MOST JEWISH

   _____

   _____

DIFFERENT AND UNIQUE

THEN & TODAY

1. Conflicts and Contradictions

As a young boy, Mordecai Kaplan had two experiences that dramatically drove home the fact that he was, and would remain, a citizen of both a Jewish and a non-Jewish world. He would always be faced with conflicts and contradictions that he would have to somehow resolve.

These conflicts and contradictions continue to face Jews today. Have you ever been confronted with a conflict between the Jewish and non-Jewish worlds in which you live? Have you ever felt pulled in two opposite directions at the same time? If so, in the space below, briefly tell what happened, how you resolved the conflict, and why? And if you have never been confronted with such a conflict or contradiction, or if you reject the idea that you are a citizen of two worlds, try to explain why.

2. "Jews Are Different"

One of the key lessons of Kaplan's childhood experiences is an idea that has been stated again and again by an odd couple that is particularly striking: the anti-Semite and the committed Jew. They both agree that Jews are different. The anti-Semite believes that this difference is somehow evil. The committed Jew insists that remaining apart is essential to the integrity of Jewish tradition, and to the creative survival of the Jewish community. In the space below write in as many ways as you can think of in which Jews are different from non-Jews.

_____

_____

_____

_____

_____

_____

Do you think that you are different from your non-Jewish friends? If so, how?

_____

_____

_____

_____

_____

Finally, is Jewish differentness something you cherish or is it a source of trouble and embarrassment to you?

_____

_____

_____

_____

_____

3. Israel's Uniqueness

It is not only Jews who are different, but the state of Israel, as well. In fact, a good case can be made for Israel's uniqueness. Can you think of ways in which Israel is a unique state and clearly not "a nation like all other nations?"

_____

_____

_____

_____

_____

RECONSTRUCTIONIST JUDAISM BELIEFS AND PRACTICES

9

A STATEMENT OF AIMS

In formulating his idea of an organic community, Kaplan set forth a number of practical suggestions, which are listed below in the left column. In the space opposite each suggestion, briefly write in what you believe is its reason. Taken together these reasons should add up to a clear, strong statement of aims of Kaplan's organic community.

SUGGESTION	REASON
1. Keep records of vital statistics	_____
	_____
	_____
	_____
	_____

2. Encourage Jews to join local and national Jewish organizations

_____
_____
_____
_____
_____

3. Set a budget for Jewish organizations to spend on Jewish needs

_____
_____
_____
_____
_____

4. Develop guidelines of ethical and moral behavior

_____
_____
_____
_____
_____

5. Strengthen Jewish education and culture

_____
_____
_____
_____
_____

6. Work to improve the health and welfare of Jews and to eliminate poverty within the Jewish community

_____
_____
_____
_____
_____

7. Encourage culture and the arts

_____
_____
_____
_____
_____

8. Fight discrimination and anti-Semitism

_____
_____
_____
_____
_____

9. Work with non-Jewish groups for the common good

_____
_____
_____
_____
_____

RECONSTRUCTIONISM AND THE COMMUNITY*

Because of its emphasis upon Jewish peoplehood, Reconstructionist Judaism judges the various movements not in terms of their religious message as such, but in terms of their contributions to the community. If a group strengthens the fabric of Jewish life, it is good. If it fails to do so, it is inadequate. Given this singular position, Reconstructionism can both compliment and criticize at the same time.

ISSUE

Compliments and Criticisms

Match each criticism of a group in the left column with a compliment of the same group in the right column. Place the number before the criticism in the blank before the matching compliment. And in the box beside each compliment, identify the group to which it refers (Orthodox, Conservative, Reform, Zionist, Secular).

CRITICISMS

COMPLIMENTS

1. "For all its achievements, it has become a bit nearsighted and narrow-minded. It is so positive that its solution is the only answer, and that if the Jewish people will only follow its leadership we can all begin to live happily ever after, that it has failed to recognize reality. The fact is, Jews will continue to live all over the world, and their needs must be recognized, respected, and dealt with effectively."

☐ "We applaud its keen sense of social conscience and the high value that it places upon personal morality. Moreover, its willingness to enter dialogues with other groups—Jewish and non-Jewish alike—has promoted a healthy measure of mutual understanding. It is also able to adapt to the present."

2. "They try so hard to straddle the fence that they become hopelessly torn and hung up between conflicting demands. The traditionalists say they compromise and sell out. And they are criticized by the changers for moving at such a snail's pace."

☐ "It firmly attests to the fact that we are first and foremost a people. Sure, religion is part of Jewish life, perhaps its most important part, but it isn't everything. In fact, there are many channels of positive involvement—historical, cultural, community service, social action, and, of course, ties with Israel."

96

3. "Everything that they do is fine and admirable, but let's not kid ourselves: Judaism is a civilization, but what gives it character and its special quality is the fact that it is a religious civilization."

☐ "There is no group that is more committed, more certain of what it stands for and where it is going, more intellectually and spiritually together. And there is such a strong sense of family and community in everything that they do: synagogue, study groups, blessings at mealtime, prayer three times a day, their celebration of the holidays and education of their children. If all Jews were like this group, there would be no assimilation."

4. "It is so self-righteous, so morally splendid, so happy to wave the flag of social conscience. Well, with due respect to goodness and compassion, high-minded ideals are not enough to preserve us. Ritual and ceremony are the glue that keeps our people together, and we'd better not forget that."

☐ "What it has achieved, against all odds, can only be described as a miracle—or indeed, a series of miracles. It has literally transformed Jewish life and given a dramatic new direction to Jewish history. For the first time in centuries, the Jewish people have a real hand in determining their own destiny."

5. "The fact is that for all of their virtues—and, from the viewpoint of Jewish survival, they have many—they are living in the Middle Ages. They are innocent of logic, ignore science, and continue to observe ancient superstitions. It's as though the eighteenth and nineteenth centuries (let alone the twentieth) had never existed."

☐ "Just as the Jewish people have had to live in two civilizations at the same time, so this group has managed to strike a delicate balance between the need to preserve the vital components of our past, while moving boldly and creatively into the future."

TRUE OR FALSE?*

1. Reconstructionism believes that Judaism is more than a religion. **T F**

2. Because it is so different from other forms of Judaism, the Reconstructionist movement keeps its distance from the Orthodox, Conservative, and Reform sectors of the Jewish community. **T F**

3. According to the Reconstructionist view, God's spirit and power must always be limited. **T F**

4. Reconstructionism believes that religion has played a crucial role in human progress. **T F**

5. Now that Jewish life has entered its democratic era—living as Jews because we choose to do so—most Reconstructionist thinkers agree that the process of change and evaluation, which has taken place throughout Jewish history, is now complete. **T F**

6. Reconstructionist Judaism believes that the major role of ritual observance is to enrich Jewish life, to strengthen its foundations, and in general, to contribute to its survival. **T F**

7. Kaplan has rejected the concept of the chosen people because he fears that it can inspire a collective superiority complex. **T F**

8. Kaplan's "new Zionism" is a product of his belief that Jewish communities around the world will continue to exist, to function, to grow, and to develop creatively. **T F**

9. A Reconstructionist prayer service, because of its democratic nature, has fewer rituals than the services of any other Jewish group. **T F**

10. Kaplan's vision of a synagogue-center is based upon his idea that Judaism is a civilization, with many ideas of interest outside of study and prayer. **T F**

COMMUNICATION

Reconstructionism is the least conventional form of Judaism, and therefore the most difficult to explain. Imagine that you are trying to communicate the meaning of the Reconstructionist approach to someone who knows little or nothing about it (there are many such people)—Jew or non-Jew. How would you explain each of the following ideas, taken from the chapter—briefly, simply, and clearly?

1. "The Bible is not the record of God's word to us but of our search for God."

2. "The past should have a vote, not a veto."

3. "Even Israeli Jews must live in Israeli civilization at the same time they live in Jewish civilization."

4. "Before the Torah can go forth from Zion, it will have to enter into Zionism."

5. "Judaism is a changing, evolving, developing *religious civilization.*"

VALUE SCRAMBLE*

Unscramble each of the words below to reveal six important values of Reconstructionist Judaism.

1. V I L I T O I C A I N Z = _____

2. M N E L F I L F U L T = _____

3. G E I L N I R O = _____

4. N I T U Y = _____

5. D I T I N I A L U Y D I V = _____

6. H E L E O D O P O P = _____

Answer the questions below briefly and clearly.

1. What does Kaplan mean when he calls Judaism a religious civilization?

   _____

   _____

   _____

   _____

   _____

2. Why does Reconstructionism reject the idea of the Jews as a chosen people?

   _____

   _____

   _____

   _____

   _____

3. What are the major elements of Kaplan's vision of a "new Zionism"?

   _____

   _____

   _____

   _____

   _____

4. On what grounds does Reconstructionism reject the Orthodox view (shared by many Conservatives and a number of Reform Jews) of God?

   _____

   _____

   _____

5. How would you explain the Reconstructionist view of God in simple terms to someone who knows nothing of the history or ideas of this movement?

_____

_____

_____

_____

6. Why have Rabbis Kaplan and Eisenstein *not* approached interfaith activities with too much enthusiasm (indeed, their attitudes could be described as hesitation bordering upon skepticism)?

_____

_____

_____

7. How does Reconstructionist Judaism justify the many differences among its members on questions of ritual observance?

_____

_____

_____

8. And why, do you think, has Mordecai Kaplan remained a strictly observant Jew throughout his life?

_____

_____

_____

JEWISH MYSTICISM AND HASIDISM VARIATIONS ON A THEME

10

A VIEW OF JEWISH MYSTICISM*

The statements below are a mix of historical perspectives and ideas growing out of this chapter's study of Jewish mysticism. Each statement contains one section that is an "outsider"—it is false. Circle the letter before the section that does not belong.

1. The history of Jewish mysticism teaches that

   a. it has been a part of Jewish life for centuries; **b.** it is based on Christian superstition and folklore; **c.** it is likely to emerge in periods of tragedy, despair, and uncertainty—when logic and reason don't seem to work; **d.** it has produced an extensive body of literature that has been carefully studied by highly respected scholars.

2. A study of the life and work of Abraham Joshua Heschel teaches that

   a. one could not be deeply involved both with mysticism, and with the social and political issues of the times; **b.** he worried about religion becoming so preoccupied with form and ceremony that it could lose its vital moral content; **c.** a man of books and ideas could also be a most effective man of action; **d.** communication between Jew and non-Jew would be valuable in many areas of experience.

3. On the subject of Israel, Heschel believed that

   a. Israel is the only place in the world where the Jew could find spiritual wholeness; **b.** there is a deep and abiding bond between the land of Israel and world Jewry; **c.** Israel is truly a holy land, to be cherished and loved; **d.** Israel's involvement with day-to-day nitty-gritty politics would destroy its unique spirituality.

4. On the question of prayer, Heschel believed that

   a. prayer is the essential language between human beings and God; **b.** prayer has to be done directly, without the services of a spiritual middleman (i.e., a professional clergyman; someone who prays on behalf of the entire congregation); **c.** prayer must be accompanied by study and ritual, or else it is not valid; **d.** prayer offers the possibility of reaching a height of spiritual joy, but our modern, secular age has made us spiritually self-conscious and "hung up," and robbed us of our ability to pray simply, sincerely, and without embarrassment.

5. According to Heschel, the Sabbath

   a. is a prime example of Judaism being rooted in time rather than in space; **b.** must be observed regularly or else it loses its meaning; **c.** points up the uniqueness and individual worth of every human being, and highlights the equality of every person before God; **d.** inspires us to cut loose from everyday ambitions, hopes, standards, and fears, and to enter a special realm of holy being, each week.

6. The Lubavitcher Hasidim

   a. draw a distinction between the accumulation of knowledge, and its application with wisdom and understanding; **b.** insist that science and religion must ultimately agree with one another because both are true; **c.** do not hesitate to use advertising and public relations techniques to bring across their message; **d.** support Israel, but only as a Torah state.

PHOTO STUDY*

Circle the number before each of the two statements that do not belong.

The photographs in this chapter (on pages 143 and 149), and their captions teach that:

1. Serious study sessions of Jewish tradition can be marked by humor and good feeling.

2. Though ultra-Orthodox Jews place extremely strict limitations upon contacts between men and women, within these boundaries communication is possible.

3. Hasidism has shown itself capable of making a positive impact not only upon those who have been brought up as Hasidim, but upon Jews whose background and lifestyle can be described as "modern American."

4. Torah scrolls must be preserved at all costs, including the sacrifice of human life, if necessary.

5. The Lubavitcher Hasidim believe that great efforts should be made to reach out even to those Jews who have abandoned their tradition and assimilated.

6. The Torah scribe is likely to be an Orthodox Jew of much dedication, professional skill, and patience.

7. The Lubavitcher Hasidim are willing to travel vast distances to strange places in order to bring their message to the Jewish people.

8. Jewish mystics regard the Torah as an object of singular holiness.

9. Although Lubavitcher Hasidim are willing to extend a spiritual helping hand to any Jew who would be redeemed, they have remained firmly and fiercely opposed to political Zionism over the years.

10. Jewish tradition demands that Torah scrolls be maintained in top shape at all times.

11. Jewish mysticism believes that the Torah is so holy that it, too, will be an important part of the world to come.

WORDS AND MEANINGS*

This chapter has a number of Hebrew words that offer important insights into the nature of Jewish mysticism. Match the meanings below with the Hebrew (and in one instance, Yiddish) words from the chapter.

1. The head of a Hasidic group, generally regarded by his followers as a saint. He has a Yiddish name, as well:

_____ or _____
(HEBREW)   (YIDDISH)

2. The part of the HaBaD "trio" which signifies knowledge (not the initial, but the whole word):

   _____

3. Jewish mysticism, as it was known in the Middle Ages, (from the Hebrew word "to receive"):

   _____

4. The state of a Torah scroll that has been restored by correcting fading or damaged letters (usually we use this word to talk about a certain kind of food):

   _____

5. The part of the HaBaD "trio" which signifies wisdom:

   _____

6. The sacred Covenant, forged between God and the Children of Israel at Mount Sinai:

   _____

7. The part of the HaBaD "trio" which signifies understanding:

   _____

8. The inner spirit which drives us, inspires us; a sense of holy purpose:

   _____

UNDERSTANDING HESCHEL

Explain each of the following quotations from the writings of Abraham Joshua Heschel as clearly as you can.

1. "A reminder of every man's royalty. . . . The greatest sin of man is to forget that he is a prince."

2. "To celebrate the Sabbath is to experience one's ultimate independence of civilization and society, of achievement and anxiety."

3. "Judaism is an attempt to prove that in order to be a man, you have to be more than a man, that in order to be a people we have to be more than a people."

4. "What is the Sabbath? . . . an abolition of the distinction of master and slave, rich and poor, success and failure."

5. "The Sabbath is holiness in time."

6. "Israel reborn is holy. . . . there can be no wholeness outside of Israel."

Support each of the following statements with a reference to, or quotation from, the text.

1. The HaBaD Hasidim possess a number of characteristics that clearly contradict one another.

_____

_____

_____

_____

2. Though steeped in tradition, the Lubavitcher movement is aware of, and sensitive to, modern thinking and methods.

_____

_____

_____

_____

3. Heschel believed that Jews must not isolate themselves, must not enclose themselves in cultural and spiritual ghettos, but, rather, must actively take part in the world around them.

_____

_____

_____

_____

4. Jewish mysticism has become popular and widely accepted in recent years.

_____

_____

_____

_____

5. Heschel believed deeply in the capacity of people to reach beyond themselves and achieve greatness.

_____

_____

_____

_____

6. Mysticism has woven its way through Jewish life and thought for centuries, and has expressed itself in a variety of ways.

_____

_____

_____

_____

IDEA SCRAMBLE*

Unscramble the groups of words below to reveal a number of major ideas in Jewish mystical thought, which have been presented in the chapter.

1. **KNOWN INNER GOD EXPERIENCES CAN THROUGH BE**

_____

_____

2. **BEING EVERY HOLY IS HUMAN**

_____

_____

3. **HAND CAN IN RELIGION GO AND SCIENCE HAND**

_____

_____

4. JEWISH MUST THE PEOPLE
   THAN MORE BE A PEOPLE

   _____
   _____

5. RELIGION OF A SPACE
   JUDAISM RATHER IS TIME
   THAN

   _____
   _____

6. SPEAK LEARN PRAYER
   GOD MUST TO PEOPLE
   THROUGH TO

   _____
   _____

7. BEFORE ALL ARE PEOPLE
   GOD EQUAL

   _____
   _____

8. CLELBRATES THE ALL
   SABBATH OF NOBILITY
   THE PEOPLE

   _____
   _____

9. TORAH THE OF PEOPLE
   MESSAGE MUST BROUGHT
   TO THE BE ALL

   _____
   _____

10. GOVERNED HOLY A ISRAEL
    WHICH TORAH BE SHOULD
    IS STATE BY THE

    _____
    _____

A COVENANT WITH TIME

THEN & TODAY

Abraham Heschel taught that Judaism is a religion of time, not just of space. When God forged Covenants with Abraham and Moses (in which we received the Land of Israel and the Torah), these were agreements also with generations that would live in the far distant future. Today when we look back on our tradition, we remember the links in the long chain of which we are a part: figures such as Moses, Samuel, Deborah, Ruth, Saul, David, Solomon, Hillel, Shammai, Maimonides, Rashi, etc. If Judaism is a religion of time, then we are a people rooted in time with a special part to play today and tomorrow.

But there are ways in which to break the Covenants, just as our ancestors did. Today these ways are many, and may include spoiling the atmosphere, polluting rivers and streams, ignoring the elderly, even forgetting our Jewish heritage.

In the chart on the next page, list some of the ways in which the world we live in (our secular world) has broken its covenant with time; and then list some of the ways in which our Jewish community has broken its covenant with time. Then, in the right hand column, think of ways in which we are keeping the covenant with time in both our secular world and our religious way of life.

111

COVENANT WITH TIME

	WAYS IN WHICH THE COVENANT IS BROKEN	WAYS IN WHICH THE COVENANT IS KEPT
SECULAR WORLD		
JEWISH WORLD		

AMERICAN JUDAISM TODAY: AN OVERVIEW

A ROUND-ROBIN REVIEW*

Identify the movement in each of the statements below.

1. The movement that believes that only the ethical mitzvot were revealed by God.

   _____

2. The movement that tries to strike a balance between tradition and change.

   _____

3. The movement that defines Judaism as a civilization.

   _____

4. The movement that most actively supports interfaith activities.

   _____

5. The movement that places the most emphasis upon the mitzvot.

   _____

6. The movement that totally rejects the idea of the Jews as a Chosen People.

_____

7. The movement that has been least involved in the area of social action.

_____

8. The movement that has the broadest range of ideas about God.

_____

9. The movement that views Judaism as a constantly unfolding, evolving historical process.

_____

10. The movement that has gone forward by looking backwards: in the direction of more awareness of history, more concern with culture and roots, more involvement with tradition.

_____

11. The movement that would like Israel to become a Torah state.

_____

12. The movement that defines God as a power or a process, rather than as a supernatural being.

_____

13. The movement that was once anti-Zionist.

_____

14. The movement that puts forth the idea of an "organic" community.

_____

15. The movement that has gone the least distance on the question of the place and participation of women within its framework.

_____

16. The two movements that believe that questions of ritual observance should be left largely up to the individual.

_____ and _____

17. The movement that will not draw a distinction between mitzvot dealing with ethics and mitzvot dealing with ritual, since—in its view—both kinds were revealed by God, and are, therefore, equally holy.

_____

18. The movement that is criticized by some for giving up certain traditions, and by others for changing too slowly.

_____

19. The movement that views the synagogue as an all-inclusive center of Jewish life.

_____

20. The movement that is credited with giving its members a firm, unquestioning faith, a sense of history, and deep, unbreakable ties with tradition.

_____

TRUE OR FALSE*

1. Reform Jews all reject the idea of a supernatural God. **T F**

2. Conservative Judaism considers ritual observance a matter of individual decision. **T F**

3. Orthodox and Reconstructionist Judaism share a suspicion of interfaith activities, and generally try to avoid them. **T F**

4. Reconstructionism believes that Israel has a special relationship with, and responsibility toward, world Jewry. **T F**

5. Conservative Judaism believes that the Torah should be Israel's national law. **T F**

6. Reconstructionists have rejected the Torah, because they do not consider it the revealed word of God. **T F**

7. The Conservative movement believes that Judaism's focal point is the Jewish people. **T F**

8. Reform Judaism looks to the prophets as a major source of inspiration. **T F**

THE REASONS WHY

1. Reform Judaism has been very active in interfaith work because

2. Orthodox Judaism digs in its heels and refuses to consider compromise on matters of tradition because

3. Reconstructionism believes that the synagogue should be an all-purpose social and cultural framework because

4. Although the Conservative movement accepts the principle of change, it moves rather slowly in this direction because

5. Conservative, Reform, and Reconstructionist Judaism have successfully struck roots in the soil of America because

A FINAL EVALUATION

Below are diagrams in which to make a final evaluation of the movements that have been presented in this book. In the spaces marked PRO list things about the movements you particularly like or admire. In the space marked CON, list things that you dislike or question. And finally, in the space marked CHANGE, write down any change or changes that you think might strengthen that movement. If you don't believe that any change is necessary, just leave a blank space—that will also say a lot.

ORTHODOX

PRO	CON

CHANGE

CONSERVATIVE

PRO	CON

CHANGE

REFORM

PRO	CON

CHANGE

RECONSTRUCTIONIST

PRO	CON

CHANGE

ANSWER KEY

This workbook has two kinds of exercises: those that can be answered by reference to facts and data in the textbook; and those that require the students to interpret the material being studied in the light of their own ideas. The following key provides answers *only* for those questions that are factual in nature.

CHAPTER ONE

A MEDIA MIX (page 2)

1. Strict immigration quotas enacted by Congress (which brought Jewish immigration to a halt), in 1926.   2. The Jewish struggle for the right to stand guard duty in New Amsterdam.   3. The trial of Dr. Lumbrozo, in Maryland   4. The arrival of Rabbi Abraham Rice, in Baltimore, the first ordained rabbi to settle in the United States.   5. Mystery event #1—the Russian pogroms and May Laws, during the 1880's; Mystery event #2—the Supreme Court decision of 1963, declaring prayer in the public schools unconstitutional; Mystery event #3—the arrival in New Amsterdam of 23 Jewish refugees from Recife, Brazil, in 1654, the first Jews to set foot in this country.

POSSIBLE OR PRECISE? (page 4)

1. d	2. e	3. b	4. a
5. c	6. d	7. c	8. e

PHOTO STUDY: TRUE OR FALSE—AND WHY?

(Here are the simple true or false answers; you supply the reasons why) (page 6)

1. True	2. True	3. False	4. True
5. False	6. False	7. True	

EVENT AND EFFECTS (page 8)

8;   7;   10;   2;   1;   9;   4;   5;   3;   6

HIDDEN WORD HUNT (page 10)

(These are the words; you find them and circle them)

1. TZEDAKAH	2. MITZVOT
3. MIKVEH	4. TREFA MEDINAH
5. KEHILLAH	6. HAZZANIM
7. SHABBAT	8. GALUT

IMMIGRANT JOURNALS (page 11)

1. E	2. H	3. S	4. H
5. W	6. E	7. H	8. W
9. S	10. E		

CHAPTER TWO

WHO, WHAT, AND WHERE, AM I? (page 14)

1. Rabbi Abraham Rice
2. B'nai Akivah
3. Yeshivah University
4. Agudat Israel
5. the sermon
6. Union of Orthodox Jewish Congregations
7. The Lubavitcher Rebbe
8. Torah Umesorah
9. Rabbi Bernard Revel and Dr. Samuel Belkin
10. The Rabbinical Council of America

HISTORICAL LESSONS (page 16)

1. c
2. b
3. d
4. a
5. b
6. a

SPECIAL MEANINGS (page 18)

1. Melamed
2. Yeshivah
3. Mitzvot
4. Semichah
5. Heder
6. Kashrut
7. Tzedakah

BETWEEN THE LINES (page 20)

4; 6; 5; 1; 2; 3

THE ORTHODOX EXPERIENCE (page 21)

1. Loneliness
2. Created a religious Zionism
3. A variety of origins
4. Open to change
5. Located in large cities
6. Built many Yeshivot

CHAPTER THREE

TRUE OR FALSE? (page 26)

1. True
2. True
3. False
4. True
5. False
6. False
7. True
8. False
9. False
10. True
11. True

ODD—IDEA OUT (page 27)

1. c
2. b
3. a
4. c
5. b
6. d
7. a

WORD AND MEANINGS (page 29)

1. Get
2. Bet Din
3. Aliyah
4. Mehitzah
5. Gedolay Hador
6. Kippah or Yarmulke
7. Siddur
8. Mohel
9. Shulhan Aruch
10. Kaddish
11. Halachah
12. Mikveh

PHOTO STUDY (page 30)

E is the letter before the statement that does not belong

WORD SCRAMBLE (page 32)

1. STUDY   2. LAND   3. PRAYER
4. FAITH   5. ETHICS   6. RITUAL
7. FAMILY

CIRCLED LETTERS: DISCIPLINE

CHAPTER FOUR

HISTORICAL LESSONS (page 34)

1. c   2. b   3. d   4. b   5. d

IDEA SCRAMBLE (page 36)

1. Judaism must become more modern. 2. The Sabbath service should have an English sermon. 3. Social justice and personal morality (or the other way around) are more important than ritual. 4. The Jewish people must strive for unity. 5. The Jewish people are a religious community but not a nation. 6. Jews should not have to pray in a language they don't understand. 7. The home is an important center of Jewish life. 8. Jewish women deserve equal status with men. 9. Judaism must be open to change. 10. Israel is a spiritual homeland for all Jews.

SPEECH—MATCHING (page 40)

4;   1;   5;   6;   3;   2

CHAPTER FIVE

(page 47)

1. True   2. True   3. False   4. True   5. False
6. False   7. True   8. False   9. True   10. True
11. False   12. True

ODD—IDEA—OUT (page 49)

1. d   2. c   3. b   4. a   5. d

WORD SCRAMBLE (page 50)

A1. BEAUTY   A2. MORALITY   A3. SPIRITUALITY
A4. CREATIVITY
B1. JUSTICE   B2. MODERNITY   B3. COMMUNITY
B4. EQUALITY   B5. FLEXIBILITY   B6. EDUCATION

CIRCLED LETTERS: SOCIAL CONSCIENCE

PLATFORM BUILDING (page 54)

The answers in this section deal *only* with the identification of platforms; you supply the reasons.

Plank #1. M   Plank #2. M and C   Plank #3. C and U
Plank #4. O and U   Plank #5. O   Plank #6. O and U
Plank #7. O, U, M, and C   Plank #8. M

CHAPTER SIX

ACHIEVEMENTS AND AWARDS (page 60)

1. Jacob Schiff
2. Dr. Louis Finkelstein
3. Rabbi Zachariah Frankel
4. Dr. Solomon Schechter
5. Rabbi Isaac Leeser
6. Rabbi Sabato Morais

HISTORICAL LESSONS (page 62)

1. b
2. c
3. d
4. c
5. a
6. b

A CYCLE OF CONSERVATIVE JEWISH LIFE (page 64)

1. The Jewish Theological Seminary
2. The Rabbinical Assembly
3. The United Synagogue of America
4. Ramah Camps
5. A tid
6. Leaders Training Fellowship
7. United Synagogue Youth
8. Solomon Schechter Day Schools

IMAGINARY SERMONS (page 66)

3;   6;   5;   2;   1;   4

CHAPTER SEVEN

TRUE OR FALSE? (page 69)

1. True
2. True
3. False
4. True
5. False
6. False
7. True
8. False
9. True
10. True

MYSTERY EDITORIALS (page 70)

The answers in this section deal *only* with the identification of the editorials; you supply the reasons.

1. R
2. C
3. C
4. O
5. R
6. O
7. O
8. C
9. R
10. C

ODD—IDEA—OUT (page 77)

1. a   2. b   3. d   4. a   5. c   6. d

HIDDEN WORD HUNT (page 79)

1. Tradition
2. History
3. Study
4. Zionism
5. Klal Yisrael
6. Dialogue
7. Compromise
8. Change

CHAPTER EIGHT

WHO, WHAT, OR WHERE, AM I? (page 80)

1. *Judaism as a Civilization*
2. The Society for the Advancement of Judaism
3. Ahas Ha-am
4. *The Reconstructionist Magazine*
5. Simon Dubnow
6. *Sabbath Prayer Book*
7. The Reconstructionist College
8. The Federation of Reconstructionist
   Congregations and Fellowships

VALUES AND VANTAGE POINTS (page 83)

The answers in this section deal *only* with "yes" or "no"; you supply the reason why.

1. yes	2. yes	3. yes	4. yes
5. yes	6. no	7. yes	8. no

EVENTS AND EFFECTS (page 87)

3;   4;   5;   6;   2;   1

IDEA SCRAMBLE (page 90)

1. Israel is the spiritual center of world Jewry. 2. Religion is a social experience. 3. The basic unit of Jewish life is the community. 4. Women must be equal participants in Jewish life. 5. Ritual observance is a source of Jewish unity. 6. The Torah is the creation of people. 7. Beliefs must be open to thoughtful examination. 8. Judaism's most important concern is the Jewish people.

CHAPTER NINE

RECONSTRUCTIONISM AND THE COMMUNITY
COMPLIMENTS AND CRITICISMS (page 96)

4;   3;   5;   1;   2
4 Reform;   3 Secular;   5 Orthodox
1 Zionist;
2 Conservative

TRUE OR FALSE? (page 98)

1. True	2. False	3. False	4. True
5. False	6. True	7. True	8. True
9. False	10. True		

VALUE SCRAMBLE (page 100)

1. CIVILIZATION	2. FULFILLMENT	3. RELIGION
4. UNITY	5. INDIVIDUALITY	6. PEOPLEHOOD

CHAPTER TEN

A VIEW OF JEWISH MYSTICISM (page 103)

1. b   2. a   3. d   4. c   5. b   6. d

PHOTO STUDY (page 104)

Statements 4 and 9 do not belong.

WORDS AND MEANINGS (page 105)

1. Tzaddik or Rebbe   2. Daat   3. Kabbalah
4. Kosher   5. Hochmah   6. Brit
7. Binah   8. Kavannah

IDEA SCRAMBLE (page 109)

1. God can be known through inner experiences.   2. Every human being is holy. 3. Science and religion can go hand in hand.   4. The Jewish people must be more than a people.   5. Judaism is a religion of time rather than space.   6. People must learn to speak to God through prayer.   7. All people are equal before God.   8. The Sabbath celebrates the nobility of all people.   9. The message of the Torah must be brought to all people.   10. Israel is a state which should be governed by the Torah.

CHAPTER ELEVEN

A ROUND—ROBIN REVIEW (page 113)

1. Reform   2. Conservative   3. Reconstructionist
4. Reform   5. Orthodox   6. Reconstructionist
7. Orthodox   8. Reform   9. Conservative
10. Reform   11. Orthodox   12. Reconstructionist
13. Reform   14. Reconstructionist 15. Orthodox
16. Reform and Reconstructionist   17. Orthodox
18. Conservative   19. Reconstructionist 20. Orthodox

TRUE OR FALSE (page 115)

1. False   2. False   3. True   4. True
5. False   6. False   7. True   8. True